I Am
Charlie
Wilson

I Am Charlie Wilson

Charlie Wilson

With Denene Millner

37INK

—

ATRIA

New York   London   Toronto   Sydney   New Delhi

ATRIA BOOKS

An Imprint of Simon & Schuster, Inc.
1230 Avenue of the Americas
New York, NY 10020

First 37 INK/Atria Books hardcover edition June 2015

37 INK/ATRIA BOOKS and colophon are trademarks of Simon & Schuster, Inc.

For information about special discounts for bulk purchases, please contact Simon & Schuster Special Sales at 1-866-506-1949 or business@simonandschuster.com

The Simon & Schuster Speakers Bureau can bring authors to your live event. For more information or to book an event, contact the Simon & Schuster Speakers Bureau at 1-866-248-3049 or visit our website at www.simonspeakers.com.

Interior design by Paul Dippolito

Manufactured in the United States of America

10   9   8   7   6   5   4   3   2   1

Library of Congress Cataloging-in-Publication Data
Wilson, Charlie, 1953–   I Am Charlie Wilson / by Charlie Wilson.
    — First 37 INK/Atria Books hardcover edition.
        pages   cm
    Includes index.
    ISBN 978-1-4767-9007-7
1. Wilson, Charlie, 1953–   2. Singers—United States—Biography.
3. Rhythm and blues musicians—United States—Biography.
I. Title.
ML420.W55267A3   2015
782.421644092—dc23
[B]   2015017804

ISBN 978-1-4767-9007-7
ISBN 978-1-4767-9009-1 (ebook)

I dedicate this book to my wife, Mahin Wilson.

I waited patiently for the LORD; and he inclined unto me, and heard my cry.

He brought me up also out of an horrible pit, out of the miry clay, and set my feet upon a rock, and established my goings.

And he hath put a new song in my mouth, even praise unto our God: many shall see it, and fear, and shall trust in the LORD.

—Psalm 40:1–3 (King James Version)

Contents

I Am
Charlie
Wilson

Prologue

Our house was very musical, but we weren't allowed to play the blues. That's what my mother would call any music that wasn't gospel—the blues. Irma Delores Wilson was saved, sanctified, and filled with the Holy Ghost, and in her mind, if you couldn't sing a particular song loudly from the front pews of the Church of God in Christ, then, like cigarettes, alcohol, and cursing, it was a sin against the good Lord. Something that would land you on the wrong side of heaven's gates.

Mind you, there wasn't any such thing as black radio in Tulsa. You had one radio station back in the fifties and sixties, and that station played Frank Sinatra, Elvis Presley, the Everly Brothers, and the like, which we could listen to occasionally when we rode in the car. But if we wanted to hear R & B music—Sam Cooke, Otis Redding, the Rolling Stones, the Temptations, the Supremes—we had to go next door for that. Miss Hanna, our neighbor, had all that music in spades, sitting right there next to one of the best-sounding stereos and speaker systems in our neighborhood. Her records were shiny, too—she kept them clean and scratch-free. My brothers, my friends, and I would sneak over there and listen to Sam Cooke's "You Send Me" and everything by Harry Belafonte. Our favorite was James Brown, a god in and of himself. He brought a whole other level of energy and soul that we could detect even at a young age. With him, you wouldn't be satisfied sitting in your chair and tapping on the counter; he was doing something completely different from that Motown romanticism—not just lyrically but musically. Motown had a heavy backbeat on the two and the four, with a tambourine attached to it. When James punched the two and the four and the horns would hit and the snap of the snare drum pounced—it was *bam!* Like gunshots. It was so powerful and monstrous you couldn't help but dance. He straightened everybody out with that funk, like, "Here I come, here I go, and here I'm going to stay." He was the leader. I was only about eight or nine when James Brown was leaving that indelible artistic mark, and every last one of my friends and I loved him with abandon. We all tried to do the "James Brown." His feet were so fast and the splits so badass. He had a hold on every young kid and teenager who ever dreamed of making music. That none of that was allowed in my house, where my father was a preacher and my mother a choir director, just made me love "the blues" even more.

Still, from the youngest age, I was so moved by this soul music, I wanted to share it with my parents. There was one artist whom I thought even they, especially my mother, could appreciate: Stevie Wonder. He moved something deep inside me. I'll never forget the first time I heard Stevie Wonder at Miss Hanna's house. He sounded like a twelve-year-old version of my mama. In fact, I thought he was a girl—rolling his voice with that same sound quality Mama had when she sang and played piano at my father's church—until somebody told me otherwise. One day when I heard "Fingertips" on the radio, I nearly lost my mind. I ran over to Miss Hanna's window and yelled out to my mother to listen, and then I turned the stereo up really high. She smiled, I snapped my fingers to the beat, and Stevie, well, he worked those licks and riffs that became part of his repertoire.

Nobody was making those runs on the radio.

Nobody.

Stevie was the first, and he was incredible. That he was a young boy, just a bit older than me, encouraged my already intense desire to sing. Prior to hearing Stevie, I didn't believe that anybody could touch the performance ability I'd displayed in church and at home and had already been getting accolades for. But there he was.

"I can get him, Mama! I can get him! I can sing like that!" I yelled.

My mother laughed. And then she got serious: "Boy, you ain't playing no blues."

Call it what you want, a sixth sense, a gut instinct, a premonition, or simply a mother's intuition, but Mama understood the trouble that could come with being a secular celebrity. The drinking. The drugs. The women. The jealousy and envy. The danger. The incredible rise and the dizzying plummets. The stakes were high. And she wanted to protect her son—a naïve, impressionable church boy—at any cost.

She did the best she could. I didn't listen. My talent, this God-given gift of vocal, performance, and musical production skills, was too strong a pull. As soon as I could, I ran toward the fire. And I got burned. In part because that is the way of the music industry: it sucks you in and, if you are not careful, chews you up into bitty pieces and spits you back out into the wind. But also because, like my mother probably knew deep down in her gut, I was not naturally endowed with all the bravado you need to navigate stardom. Not in the earliest of my days in the spotlight, anyway.

My friend Rick James, whom I'd meet after my family band, The GAP Band, started making it, knew this, too. He used to tell me that I was much too quiet. Rick was boisterously charismatic, the way he walked, the way he commanded a room. When I met him in 1978 or 1979, he was already a bona fide rock star and was covering some of The GAP Band's music in his shows. He was on the Motown label, so he had a machine in his corner. He also had the Stone City Band up there onstage with him and a fan base that got downright rabid from the moment he'd come out, shirtless, into the spotlight, the tails of his long leather coat flying behind him, his man tights and leg warmers sitting funky in his cowboy boots, and all that hair swinging past his shoulders. When his fingers got to prancing across the strings of his guitar and the audience made out the notes for the intro to "You and I" or caught wind of the opening licks to "Mary Jane," the entire arena would combust into all kinds of screaming and shouting and frenetic energy. Rick James was electric, and he was drawn to me because I was his complement onstage—wild and full of bravado. Active. He liked that. He liked me. And pretty quickly after we met, we were fast friends, running the streets and hitting the clubs and getting into all kinds of debauchery together. But it was hard for me to keep up with Rick.

One night he had me ride in the limo with him and an entourage of about ten people as we headed for the China Club in Los Angeles. Rick was practically talking in tongues—"All you gappers and finger snappers and toe tappers and you love rappers," that line from The GAP Band's "I Don't Believe You Want to Get Up and Dance (Oops!)," was just one of the jewels Rick dropped that night in the limo—and to say he was amped when it came time to walk past the velvet rope and into the doors of the China Club would be an understatement. I was by his side in the car, but by the time all the people piled out of that limo and the bodyguards started jumping out of their cars and the swag level of Rick James and his entourage was turned up to one thousand, I was all the way in the back of the line, having been shoved out of the way by Rick's various groupies and clingers-on as they jockeyed for space in his orbit.

That's the way I was: Vibrant onstage but quiet and unassuming off. Too afraid to speak up. Rick was a superstar. Me, I was just the lead singer in a band. "You're too humble," Rick said to me when we finally found each other in the VIP room after twenty minutes. I didn't want to cause a scene or be a problem to anybody, and he wanted me to be the opposite. "You should have been right here next to me the whole time."

"How could I do that?" I asked. "I had people pushing me out the way."

"You gotta act like a star," he said, tossing in a few curse words to put an exclamation mark on his point. "Watch me. I'll show you how."

The next day, he dressed me up in all this stuff—all that Rick James accouterment that made him bigger than life: boots and tights, leather, and leg warmers. And he had me walking around with him like that—trying to give me a different swagger. "Who are you?" he kept asking me. "I know who I am. The name is Rick James, bitch." That was not a saying made up by Charlie Murphy and Dave Chappelle for a TV skit. Rick was really like that. That was his thing: "This is rock and roll, bitch." He insisted I say it, but I couldn't do it. Having been raised in a preacher's house, I couldn't see myself responding to someone who asked me my name with a "My name is Charlie Wilson, bitch!" So I didn't say it, I didn't think it, I didn't act on it. I didn't run through the women and call them bitches. I just let Rick act on it. And that was okay for a minute, but after a while, I started feeling less than—as if I were the clinger-on and everyone else was the superstar. I felt little. Belittled. Rick, Sly, Stevie Wonder, all the superstars I hung with had everything, and there I was with so little self-esteem. I felt as if I were a nothing, had nothing. Then soon enough, that nothing manifested for real.

Low self-esteem was the bitch.

And ultimately, the catalyst for my spectacular downfall.

Singing the blues didn't kill me after all. Music, my gift, helped me to soar, dropped me to my lowest of lows, and resurrected me in ways immeasurable. In fact, it, along with God's goodness and mercy, imprinted on me as a child raised by the hand of a woman who loved and revered the Lord, saved my life.

Chapter 1

Becoming Charlie Wilson

My daddy was a preacher with that Bible-thumping, Southern Baptist fire deep in his bones. That early-Sunday-morning vigor gave him wings; he'd fly all over that pulpit and all through the church, crowing through the pews and hopping over laps, the Word dripping from his tongue. That man could jump three or four feet in the air, and by the time he made it back down, people were falling out and shouting. I'm not going to lie: my daddy's hollering and screaming scared me. The way the congregants of the Church of God in Christ in Tulsa, Oklahoma, would jump in the rhythm and work themselves into a frenzy was confusing. Alarming. Addictive.

I was about four years old when I said, "I want to do that." My father happily obliged me, seeing as my oldest brother, Ronnie, and later my sister, Loretta, both gave up their position as the good pastor's warm-up act when they turned twelve and got a little too much preteen angst to be bothered. I had no problems handling the gig.

I took my cues from my father.

Oscar Wilson was a boy preacher. A prodigy. At just thirteen years old, he took off from his home in Lehigh, Oklahoma, in the dead of night with nothing but a small suitcase and a Bible, chasing behind God's voice and a light that lit his footpath through the pitch dark. The Lord had spoken to him—told him to get on the first train coming and ride it through the countryside until He told him where to get off. The average teenager may have thought he was going slowly, surely mad, following behind a voice that insisted he leave all he knew and deposit himself on a locomotive, destination unknown. But when my father heard the calling, he listened. He ended up a few stops down that stretch of railroad track, in a small town with a huge, empty field God directed him to. When he arrived there sans a chaperone, the people there said, "What's your name?"

"Oscar Wilson," I'm told he replied.

"Wilson, huh," one man stated. "What's your daddy's name?"

"Dave Wilson," my father answered.

"Boy, you Dave Wilson's son?" another man asked.

"Yessir," my father answered quickly, understanding the cachet this carried in this town among its people, both of which were foreign to him. My grandfather, Dave, was somewhat of a pistol. Literally. I'm told that he was a full-blooded Indian with a hot temper and an itchy trigger finger. Word has it that he once shot the town sheriff and got away with it, and that he was known for lying in the road with his Winchester rifle, waiting for someone to say something sideways to him. After that incident with the sheriff, no one ever did. His reputation preceded him. "Dave's lying across the road with that Winchester," they'd warn anyone who approached. "Be careful."

So when my father showed up talking about preaching, the townspeople, either impressed or out of fear, happily obliged him, strange as his intentions were. "Where you going to preach?" they asked him.

"Right in that field over there," he stated matter-of-factly. "That's where God told me to preach."

They made my father a little platform and strung up some lights for him so that the people could see him. He preached to a few people on the first night and to double that number the second night, and bit by bit, hundreds and hundreds of people showed up to hear the boy preacher. He was answering God's calling, and the people were getting saved. An evangelist, my father preached all around the country for most of his years on this here earth.

I honed my stage presence and singing performances in the back room of my childhood home, in front of the mirror, where I would mimic my daddy and my mama's church preaching and praise. When people see me whirling across the stage with all that infectious energy and ask me where I learned to perform, without hesitation, I give that credit to my father. When he was in the pulpit, Daddy would sing and shout all kinds of things, like, "Throw your hands in the air!" and "Say yeah!" while my mother was over there getting down on that piano, whipping him and the entire congregation into a frenzy. Those are move-the-crowd standards that I tend to shout out during my concerts, even today, but I've been working on and perfecting my high-energy stage exploits for a lifetime. It wasn't a thing for my family to open the door and see four-year-old me wrapped in one of my mother's robes, my father's shoes flopping off of my tiny feet, flying through the air, landing in front of a mirror: "He's a mind regulator and a mind fixer and a burden bearer!" I'd be shouting, jumping, twisting, squalling, rearing back, and playing the air piano, all at the same time. My parents would take a gander at the dramatics in that back room and just shake their heads. "Boy, we got our hands full with this one," they'd say, laughing. Of course, because our house was deeply religious, it wasn't strange to anyone that a four-year-old was preaching and jumping and shouting at his own reflection. It was expected.

There were more dramatics on Sunday when I put my routine into action at the church. Dress code: blue gabardine suit jacket with matching shorts and bow tie. The song: "When They Ring the Golden Bells." Nerves: nonexistent. There was no reason to be scared; we grew up in the church, quite literally, spending at least three days out of the week, sometimes more, learning both the Bible and how to be. At any point in time, you could be standing up in front of the entire Sunday school to recite Bible verses you learned in class, or playing a baby lamb in the Nativity play at Christmas, or spending the entire Saturday with your church friends and their parents, doing good works out in the community or dancing and playing at the congregation's picnic. Being in front of one another, fellowshipping and growing, is what we kids did in the church, and everybody embraced you, no matter what you did or how you did it. Even if you couldn't sing or you got a few of the words in that verse jumbled, everybody would get up on their feet and clap for you so that you knew you were loved, and when there is love, there is no guard—no wall. You show up, open your mouth, and sing. Of course, it helped, too, that my mother insisted we Wilson kids were the best singers. But really, everybody—the crooners and the croakers—could stand up in front of a microphone and be made to feel as if they'd turned the place out. There was nothing to get nervous about at all. Plus, when it came time for my solo, Mama had already practiced the song with me, and on top of that, I was on a mission: my father delivered a powerful sermon every Sunday and it was my job to make sure the spirit was high and everybody within range of the sound of my voice was in full-on shout mode. My voice may have been sweet and pure and the scab on my knee may have betrayed just how little and new I was, but that old soul deep in my bones had crept up through my center mass and into my throat and was waiting there like a revving race car at the starting line. My mom was sitting at the big upright piano, with my siblings and me standing off to the side of her. "It's time to sing, baby," she said, nodding at me.

Let me tell you, when she put that microphone in my hand? I took off—headed straight for the pulpit, where the preachers and deacons were. And when I rounded that corner and saw my daddy, he stood up and then everybody else did, too, and I knew that was my cue. *I went in.* I started shouting and moved down the aisle as far as I could get with that microphone, jumping and throwing my leg up and my head all the way back. People were going crazy and shouting with joy, and by the time I finished, my dad got up humming, happy I'd warmed up the congregation, yes, but also proud that his son was hopping in his footsteps.

My addiction to that energy, that power over an audience, extended beyond the church pews, right into the halls of Dunbar Elementary School. My brother and sister had already been through the school, so I walked in there with a serious rep. I was "Little Wilson," the teacher's pet. They had me singing on demand: the instructors would say, "Come here, Little Wilson. Let me see if you can sing this song." I'd get the song's key and dive in. The response they'd give was inevitably along the lines of, "Oh my gosh, what a beautiful voice," whenever I sang.

That much I could handle, but I wasn't ready for what would happen once I shared my abilities with a bigger school audience. Indeed, I got the full brunt of people's response to my singing at a talent show, when I was in the fourth grade. Someone taught me Tony Bennett's signature song, "I Left My Heart in San Francisco," and I sang it in front of an auditorium packed with my elementary school peers. As I sang, they began to scream and swoon as if I were Frankie Valli. And when those last words crossed my lips—"Your golden sun will shine for me"—those girls came running toward me full-speed, screaming and waving their hands in the air. A good eighty to one hundred of them. I still had my arm in the air and my eyes closed, dragging out that last note, when I heard the stampede. It scared me so much I took off running! With the entire elementary school of girls chasing me, I scrambled off the stage and down the hallways, searching desperately for an escape; I pushed through the first door I could find, not sure what to do or how to survive a gaggle of screaming fourth-, fifth-, and sixth-grade little girls. Big mistake. I didn't realize what the room was until I saw the stalls: the girls' bathroom. I was trapped. Shaking, I almost peed my pants when a teacher pulled me out of there and rushed me into another room.

"You all right, Charles?" the teacher asked, brushing off my clothes and putting her hands on my shoulders to steady me. Breathing hard, I held back the tears, completely traumatized.

． ． ．

That teacher pulled me into the teachers' lounge, away from the grabby hands and shrieks of my peers, tucked away safe until, finally, my mother got there. When she walked into the room, I could tell she was trying her hardest to suppress her laughter. "Your little heart is beating so fast," she said between stifled giggles.

My mother couldn't wait to tell my daddy the story when we got home. "Babe, they ran him into the bathroom. One of the teachers had him over there in a separate room and the halls were full of kids trying to get to him," she said, her laughter met with my father's easy grin. My mom hugged me and said in that soothing voice: "It's okay, baby. You did good. You did *real* good."

That had never happened to me before. Once I recovered, I realized I liked it. A lot. From then on, anytime anything needed to be sung at the school, I was the chosen one. And I was always ready for the reaction. I was pretty all right with the girls chasing me after that; the sixth graders wanted to kiss me all the time. I craved that excitement and would look for it anywhere I could—on the stage, and later, in everything from my relationships, to my career, to even my addictions. I understood instinctively, even at age six, that the sound of the crowd is life.

My air.

Chapter 2

Music, Family, Heartbreak

My musical talent must have a genetic component. My mom's brother played piano; my father played a little guitar; my brother Ronnie played drums, piano, and coronet; and we all played a little violin because that's what you started playing in school as a young student, when learning an instrument was mandatory. It sounded like we were strangling cats, but my mother thought it was beautiful. All of us—my older siblings, Ronnie and Loretta, and my younger brother, Robert, and I—could sing. God gifted us with it. But it was my mother who was the most talented of all. Killer on the piano, she could play really fast with both hands—one hand playing one chord structure, the other doing something totally different. She had a particular talent for songs that dancers would perform the Lindy Hop to, the dance where a man slings his partner up his side and into the air. Those fingers could fly! I grew up hearing tales that Ray Charles and some of the other popular singers of the time heard my mom play and tried their hardest to get her to join their bands, but my grandmother would have none of that. Maybe she knew what everyone else did: that singing that doo-wop secular music was sending all too many of our most popular musicians, Ray Charles included, down a spiraling hole of drug dependency, prison, and ruined lives. So whenever anyone asked my mother to play secular music, she would tell him, "I'm saved and sanctified and filled with the Holy Ghost. I can't do that."

She did play for the church, though. Everybody loved Sister Wilson. My mom was the state minister of music Oklahoma North West, meaning she organized all the state choirs, featuring singers from all different churches around that region of Oklahoma. Whenever there was a convocation or a big revival somewhere, or some bishop was being celebrated, they would put all the church singing groups in one mass choir and my mother would lead it—picking out the music, the musicians, the lead singers, the wardrobe, right on down to choreography. Everything that went on musically in our state had to go through her.

Of course, she also played for my dad, who was by then a preacher at the Church of God in Christ in Sand Springs, Oklahoma, near where I grew up. Though I have only scant details on how they met, I have no doubt that church was involved, with my father in the pulpit and my mother conjuring up the ghost on that piano.

It was my mother who taught me how to play the trumpet and the piano. I wanted to play those instruments because my older brother, Ronnie, was playing them. When I expressed my desire to play to my mother, she said, "Okay, baby, go get the horn." When I brought it to her, she put it right up to her lips and said, "Hold your mouth like this." I'd never seen a woman, let alone my mother, play a trumpet before.

"Mama, you play trumpet, too?" I asked, shocked but excited.

Turns out that in high school back in her hometown of Ada, Oklahoma, she was a first-chair trumpet player! She taught us all how to play brass instruments, and the piano, which she taught to other kids in the neighborhood, too. When I realized that she was teaching others, I was surprised because I didn't even know she knew how to read music. In church, she wouldn't use sheet music because she had memorized the songs. But one afternoon, I came home from school and there were students tumbling out of the door. When I went into the piano room, she was in there reading music, transforming the chord structure of a hymn to make it sound more like a gospel song. Right then, I asked if she could teach me how to do that. She sat me down and showed me how to read the notes and gave me something to play. I proceeded to do so without looking at the sheet music; I could just hear and feel what was supposed to come next and I played it.

"You're not reading the music, Charles," she said. "You're mimicking what I'm playing."

Always, I could play by ear. The ability to feel the music, to move it beyond what is on the paper, is the ultimate gift, one that, to this day, serves me well when I'm in the studio with colleagues—producers, musicians, and artists, alike—who usually have no idea that when it comes to the music, I can do much more than simply sing.

. . .

My mother's instruction was inspiring but I found her repertoire limiting. She forbade me from singing secular music but that didn't stop me from wanting to, especially when I got a gander at my father's nephew. Lowell Fulson was a blues singer. He had written a song called "Tramp" and he was famous around the fifties and sixties. Light-skinned, like my father, with a dimple to boot, he used to come to our house with his hair all shiny, driving a great big old car that was even shinier—a Cadillac, as I recall—and with gold teeth that added a sparkle to it all. I saw him and said, "Man, that's what I want to be."

I thank God my parents nurtured this gift my siblings and I shared. It would have been just as easy for them to tamp down their kids' desire to lead lives filled with music, particularly in a household led by a Holy Roller who thought the kinds of noise we wanted to make with our voices and instruments were the source of the devil's temptations. But that wasn't the way of Oscar and Irma Wilson. There we were, right there in Tulsa, Oklahoma, in the middle of segregation, Jim Crow, and the burgeoning civil rights movement, and my parents were right by our side, focusing not on the system of racist laws that dictated what we *couldn't* have but all the things they could give us within a rigid, constricted system that relegated black people to second-tier schools, housing, and social opportunities: a sound education; time for any extracurricular activity we had an interest in, including marching band, football, and basketball; and a solid religious foundation that fed us spiritually, emotionally, and socially. Of course, because we were African-Americans in a country that purposefully tried to restrict us based on the color of our skin, we weren't immune to the foolishness of the times; we had our moments when race tainted our everyday interactions: there were "colored" and "whites only" water fountains and a segregated and unequal school system; there were times when I, a child, was referred to as "nigger boy," a name I simply could not comprehend; and in our community, there were always memories of the 1921 Tulsa race riots, which killed countless innocent black Oklahomans and destroyed the prominent Greenwood Avenue community known as "Black Wall Street." This history was never far from any of our minds.

I remember vividly one time, when I was about five or so, going to Woolworth's with my parents and running through the front doors of the store, headed straight for the stand where they served up strawberry malts. I didn't know what "whites only" meant or that there was a door in the back reserved for people with my skin color; I just knew that if I deposited myself on the little bar stool at the counter, I'd be in prime position to get me one of those malts. So, without hesitation, when my father pulled his car up in front of the store, I jumped out and went running through the doors and hopped right on up onto that stool and started spinning around and around. And oh my gosh, I heard my mother hollering out to me, frantic, but I didn't pay her any mind because I was getting myself ready for that malt. To be honest, I didn't even really understand why the man in the white outfit and the little white hat was yelling or what he meant when he said, "Come get this little nigger bastard," or why he was making his way from behind the counter, but my mom sure did make it plain when she came rushing through the doors and yelled, "Don't you do it! If you hit him, you're going to draw back a nub!" My mama was reaching into her purse as that man got closer to me. I didn't know what his intentions were, but my parents did. That man was aiming to hit me.

My mother and he were going at it, yelling and scream-ing at each other—him calling me and my mama all kinds of "nigger bastards," my mama telling him he better not touch her child—when my father came in through the "colored" en-trance in the back. "In the name of God, don't you do it," I heard his voice boom.

That man kept right on yelling. I'll never know what he was thinking, but I know this much: he didn't touch me or my mother. My mother had given him just the right amount of crazy and my father just the right amount of authority to make that man understand his place when it came to me—that no matter what the laws said, no matter what his beliefs directed him to do, he had no right to put his hands on me. If he did, there would be hell to pay.

That was a traumatizing moment. One I'll never forget. Still, my parents didn't dwell on the inequities and neither did I. Instead, we looked to what was good in the community. We lived across the street and next door to places owned and run by white people who were kind to us. Mr. Reynolds, who owned the business opposite our house, let us kids hole up in his basement when the tornadoes would storm through Tulsa. There would be a foot of water in that basement, but there we'd be, standing there, safe from the destruction. Mr. Reynolds never called us names—never talked to us in an unkind way. The same for Miss Hanna, the woman next door who would let me listen to Stevie Wonder and James Brown on her ste-reo and pour us tall glasses of iced Kool-Aid when it was hotter than the Fourth of July. They cared for us the way neighbors did back then.

That's the way I experienced life in Tulsa. It was easy, pure fun, with my parents nurturing my brothers and sister and me, indulging our passions and exposing us to the art of music and performance. We led fulfilled lives.

All of that changed suddenly, tragically, heartbreakingly, when I was just thirteen years old. That was when my father up and left our family. To be blunt about it, my father was a looker—a God-fearing preacher with a wandering eye who eventually became what the Temptations referred to as a "rolling stone."

He loved my mom and they stayed together for about seventeen years; there's something to be said for that. But while my mother never, ever did anything that would tarnish their marriage, my father was not a perfect man. Though I didn't understand just how rocky their relationship was until I was about twelve years old or so—old enough not only to see what was going on but to reasonably understand it—I now know that my father had put my mother through some tough situations for quite some time. I remember her searching his pockets and screaming at him in the car with that loud, boisterous, signature holler that the Collins side of the family is known for. I recall, too, the few times he would give one of the congregants a lift home from church with all us kids in the car, and how he would tell us to go to the back of her house to see if the door was open, and how stupid we must have looked back there tugging on that knob while he was in the car, doing whatever it was he did with this woman when they had a few minutes alone. Today, it makes me feel dumb to have been so gullible. And angry that it was so easy for him to leave us—to leave me.

I didn't get firsthand the reason why my father left, but I'm told by one of my brothers that just as my father was on track to become a bishop in our church, his mistress announced that she was pregnant. This, of course, would have destroyed his standing in the church, and devastated my mother and what they had. Instead of standing up to face what he'd done, he and his lady bounced. I'm not sure what he said to my mother when he left. What I do know is that he left without saying good-bye to me.

This came after he gave me one of the worst whoopings I'd ever gotten. I had it coming. I was really starting to be something else—smoking and drinking, hanging with a fast crowd, doing what teenagers do when they start getting full of themselves. On this one particular Saturday night, I was out with my friends and didn't bother coming home until around the time my father was heading to church. Dad was in the car with another preacher when I walked up, and I swear I could see the fire in his eyes.

"Get on in that house, boy!" he yelled through the car window. "I'll deal with you when I get back."

Oh my, was my father upset! But that didn't make me pay any mind; when he got back, I was gone again—out drinking and smoking cigarettes. Out there, I was being pulled from left to right, learning things I shouldn't have been learning at such a young age but taking it all in nevertheless, because as a preacher's child who had gone to church no less than three days a week my whole life, and who had lived under the supervision of a mom who watched me so closely, all I wanted to do was to get out from up under that yoke and try some things—to experiment and do exactly what everyone said I shouldn't do.

When I came back home, it was about two in the morning. I knocked on the back door so that my brother could sneak me in, but he wouldn't open up the door for me. I had no other choice but to go through the front, where my mother was waiting for me. She started whaling on me with a little dress belt; it didn't hurt, but I acted like it did because I didn't want my father to come into the room and get a piece of that action.

"Okay, okay, I won't do it again," I whisper-yelled, forcing tears to my eyes for dramatic effect.

"You better not," she said, winded.

Then I heard the bed creaking. My father was awake and headed for the living room with *his* belt. And when he rushed in, he whipped me and whipped me and *whipped* me. Everybody started coming out of their bedrooms, rubbing their eyes, groggy but scared for their brother. Finally, my mother said, "Okay, Rev, that's enough."

With the licks of that belt still burning my flesh, I looked right at my father and, with everything I had in me, I said, "I hate you. *I hate you*," and ran out the back door.

A few days later, on the third of July, he was gone.

I thought I was the reason he left. But I was counting on his coming back, particularly since it was July 4, which was a big holiday for us; there'd be barbecue and drinks and lots of fireworks. Each of us had our own supply of firecrackers and bottle rockets and sparklers. My brothers and sister set off their provisions all throughout the day and into the night, but I just sat there on the porch, waiting for my father to come home so that we could light mine together.

It was nightfall when I realized the gravity of the situation:

Daddy was gone. Finally, as midnight fast approached, my mother came out onto the stoop and put an end to the waiting: "Boy, you better pop those firecrackers and come on in here into this house," she said. She didn't have to say my father wasn't coming back that night. I didn't know all his clothes were gone. But I had a feeling—knew it deep down. Sometime just before midnight, disappointed, I went out there and lit the whole pack of firecrackers and shot everything off in a matter of five minutes. I'd never felt more alone than I did in those moments. Once I realized my father was gone for good, I went on a downward spiral.

.　.　.

My dad had left the city; he moved with his mistress to Denver, continuing his evangelist work, traveling from church to church and city to city without ever coming back home to see us kids. My mom was left to be a single mom, raising me, my sister, and my little brother, and relying on my older brother—he was married and already living outside our home with his wife—to talk to me when I got out of pocket. But I wasn't trying to hear anything he, my mother, or anybody else had to say. I was newly belligerent. I'd argue with my mom and anyone else in my path. Fueled by my anger with my dad, I was out of control. My brothers and my sister were devastated by my father's absence, but in my own mind, in my own world, I was beyond that. I was bitter.

Meanwhile, the marriages of my friends' parents remained intact. I would go by my friends' homes and be in agony when I saw fathers and mothers together in that really wholesome family kind of way. Whatever the guys would do, their parents would be there, keys in hand, ready to take us all where we needed to go and happy to support us in whatever it was we were getting into at the time.

By the time my mother sent me off to stay with my dad for a while, I was too far gone—too incredibly angry with him and his new wife—for him to do me any good. I shake my head now with remorse when I think about how much like an ass I was when I lived with him. If it snowed, I'd walk in the snow and mud just so that I could stomp back in the house and put my wet, muddy feet on their coffee table. I'd do anything and everything possible to provoke them into saying something to me so that I could go buck-wild up in their house—really let out all the rage I had built up inside me.

I ended up back home with my mom, and my dad called a little less frequently until he went for days without talking to me and then weeks and then months, until finally, I didn't see or hear from him anymore. Not for a long time.

Instead, I watched my mom cry a lot.

Mind you, I come from a generation that didn't really do all that talking and checking in with the kids and evaluating their feelings and figuring out how they were faring in the midst of stress and strife. I come from a time where children were to be seen, not heard, and only the grown-ups were privy to grownfolk business. Anybody who wasn't grown? They were left to try to work out what was going on in the house in their own way, and if that stress manifested itself in negative behavior—lashing out, breaking rules, doing poorly in school—nobody really stepped in and tried to help them deal with it. I think my parents figured they had enough problems to try to hash out on their own without stopping to try to figure out whether we kids were okay. There were four of us, and though my brother Ronnie was in a place of his own, my mother was still charged with raising three teenagers by herself; she had her eye on my sister, trying to make sure there weren't any boys coming in the house; she was dealing with my hormones and teenage rage; and she was watching my little brother, working to make sure he was staying out of the trouble that seemed to be swallowing me whole.

The one thing that brought me peace—the thing that brought me joy—was music. Singing, playing, performing.

Chapter 3

Greenwood, Archer, and Pine

I can't say that my big brother, Ronnie, was my hero. We loved each other, sure; this is the way of brothers. But our relationship was pretty prickly when I was a kid and he exercised his authority over me. Of course, battles between siblings are as old as the story of Cain and Abel—as epic as the rivalry between Cinderella and her stepsisters. But when you're catching hell on the other end of your big brother's fist, really, you're not thinking about Bible stories and fairy tales; you're trying to dodge the wrath. My brother Ronnie brought that in spades. He *terrorized* me. From when I was around age eight and he was a teenager with seven years, several inches, and about fifty pounds on me, it would go down practically before my parents could get out of the front door and down the steps as they left the house en route to work. Ronnie would pounce on me like a clever, fast cat on a tiny mouse. Punches to the gut. Slaps across the cheeks. Shoving. Tripping. He'd hold me down and let saliva drip from his lips slow and sticky, slithering within centimeters of my face, then suck it up just before the spit connected with my skin. It was terrifying for this then-eight-year-old, who just didn't know what to expect when the grown-ups were gone. He'd even light into me first thing in the morning, when my parents would send him to wake me up. It'd be *pow!*, right to the head. I'd start hollering and crying, and my parents would come to that back room to see what all the commotion was about, and Ronnie would get real slick with it: "Mama, come on," he'd say. "I'm not anywhere near him. He's just screaming for nothing." Just the sound of his voice would send fear down my spine.

My sister, Loretta, on the other hand, had my back. If someone was coming for me, our brother included, she would transform into my own personal Superwoman and put the smackdown on them—and even take a punch or two of her own to keep her little brother, two years her junior, from harm. One time, when a huge fight broke out during a student gathering at the YMCA and some guy in the middle of the melee started toward me with his fists balled up, Loretta hit him right across the head with a glass bottle. Yes, Loretta had my back. Of the four Wilson siblings, she and I were the closest. And it pleased me to follow in her footsteps. She could play the piano and sing— she was bad, too! To this day, she has a beautiful voice—strong, confident. Distinctly Wilson. When she was about to leave elementary school for junior high, she spent the last sixteen months letting everybody, from the students to the teachers, know that her little brother was on the scene. I'd encounter the same reaction time and again. "Oh, you're Loretta and Ronnie's little brother. Can you sing like your sister or your brother?" And I wouldn't hesitate to bust a little tune. "Oh my gosh, this one has a beautiful voice," they would say. "Like heaven." And because of her, I drew more favor with the teachers, too. They would let me have the run of the music class whenever I, Little Wilson, stepped into the room. One music teacher was especially benevolent. After you spent the year learning how to scratch out "Twinkle, Twinkle, Little Star" on the violin, you could pick the instrument you wanted to play. I didn't want to wait around for all of that; I had my eyes on the drums and the trumpet and I wanted to learn all three instruments at the same time, if I could. One morning, I eagerly showed the instructor what I could do; I had that "Twinkle" down pat, and before I could firmly put that violin down, I was practically doing the James Brown while making my pitch to move on to bigger, better instruments.

"You related to Ronnie and Loretta?" the instructor asked, choking back laughter.

"Yes!" I said, nodding furiously.

"I knew it! I can't just let you play what you want to play in this class with everybody else playing the one instrument," he said. "But I'll tell you what: you stick with the violin, and before the season is up, you can play other things." And if anybody tried to make a fuss about it, he and all the other teachers had my back. "He's more advanced," they'd say as they'd hand me another instrument to try out. These days, with school music programs across the country being obliterated in budget cuts, kids who could have the musical gifts of a Charlie Wilson or a Stevie Wonder, Justin Timberlake, Pharrell, or Alicia Keys are being denied access to even the basic music lessons that were standard back in my day, and that's the shame of it all. I wasn't out gangbanging or getting into that much trouble; there was always music for me. More, my family, my teachers, and other adults in my church and community supported my love for song. But these days, kids who might love to learn an instrument but have no outlet or opportunity to do so truly are missing out.

We had only a short time at junior high together, but by the time we met up there, Loretta and I were tearing it up. We'd sign up for the talent shows and wreck the place. Anything by Marvin Gaye and Tammi Terrell were our signature duets. It was the same when she moved on to high school; my sister was really popular and I took great pride being invited to hang tough with her and all her high school friends, and she would look out for me, making sure I was protected. When it came to my singing, I was following in a good smoking trail behind her, for sure.

Though I didn't mess with Ronnie, I did look up to him when it came to what he was doing musically. He had his musical crew, but I had mine, too, and by seventh grade, all my friends, who loved music as much as I did, and I put together our own band and started playing. The Supremes, Stevie Wonder, the Beatles, Wilson Pickett, James Brown, the Rolling Stones—all of them were spinning on record players all around Tulsa, and my boys and I were obsessed with learning and replicating every single note, turn of phrase, inflection, and dance move the best of the best had to offer on the Top 100 charts. We were beasts at it, too—just as good as my brother. Younger and a lot cuter, but just as good.

We started out as the Carver GTs, named for our school, George Washington Carver Middle School. I was on trumpet, and our band had a trombonist, a guitarist, a guy on the bass, and a drummer. We played all kinds of things—just jammed—

and then one of us would hop off his instrument and do the James Brown with the split and the squall. Everybody would lose their mind. We were a heck of a band. And that band turned into a second incarnation we called the Spinatas, after that super-sweet, fruity wine everybody was drinking back then. We would have so much fun—there were no rules other than learning the song, rotating the instruments when we wanted to, taking turns on vocals, and playing. I know that when my band members and I were little, we each dreamed of being what most kids dream of being—a doctor or a lawyer, a fireman or a police-man. But when we discovered music, we each fell in love, and I knew that there was nothing else in the cards for me but to be an artist. After school, we would go to the restrooms, where the acoustics were better, and blow our horns and rap out taps on the tile walls and sinks and listen to our voices bounce around the room. One of our favorite songs to play was "Bugler's Hol-iday," a piece for trumpet trio that required double and triple tonguing. When we saw my brother and his boys playing it at a high school function, we memorized the tune and stayed in the bathroom playing what we thought we'd learned. By the time we got to high school, nobody else in the band could play it but us and our teacher, and when we finally got the sheet music and read the notes, it was over for everybody. Nobody could touch us! That's how we were, though: passionate.

There were other pursuits, sure. I was quite the athlete—pretty good at basketball and football, too. I lived in the gym: I would go there after school, just before we headed over to a club called A Blue Monday to play; shoot the ball from anywhere on the court; then head back into the locker room, change my clothes, grab my trumpet, and get on down the street. We didn't lose much. In fact, we were so good even when we were just elementary school players that we banded together as the Y Little Five and scored thirty-three points against grown-ups. I mean, they beat us 130 to 33, but still, we were nine-year-olds scoring against adults.

We kept playing through junior high and high school, but I didn't care for my high school coach. Before he came to us, he was the coach of our archrival in junior high school, and I hated playing against him because whenever I got close, I could smell alcohol on his breath. We used to make fun of that team for it, too: "Y'all got a drunk coach!" we'd taunt. When I found out he was our new high school coach, I announced with great authority that I wasn't about to play for him. "Man, that's that drunk right there!" I yelled.

I didn't fare much better come junior high football. I could catch anything they threw to me and I was good at my job as free safety, especially intercepting the ball. But during one particularly rough game, I got slaughtered by the opposition, which set me up to be manhandled as if I'd stolen something from the coach's mama. Someone threw the ball to my side and when I went up to intercept it, it seemed as if the entire team came for me. I tucked my head into my shoulder pad and took the worst hit anybody could have ever doled out on a high school football field. All I saw was sky, ground, sky, ground, sky, ground, and then black. They knocked me out cold. When I came to, little girls were on the sidelines crying. They thought I was dead. After that, no more football for me. I gave up sports for the music.

After a while, we got good enough to play gigs at the local

YMCA. Our fellow students would pay forty-five cents to get in and we would play, under the supervision of chaperones, all the latest songs—Stevie's "Uptight (Everything's Alright)," Aretha Franklin's "Respect," James Brown's "Papa's Got a Brand New Bag," and all that Stax/Memphis soul Booker T and the MGs were laying down on wax. We were even mimicking my brother Ronnie's band—we'd watch them rehearse and perform all those popular songs and then go right back to our "studio" to learn it all and play it exactly like we heard it.

By the time we got to be sophomores in high school, the Spinatas were good enough to move from the YMCA to A Blue Monday. And you know who was partying at that club? All the twenty- and thirtysomething grown-ups who used to chaperone us at the Y, plus even some of our teachers and the school principal. There they were drinking and dancing and hooking up, and, yes, some of them would be indulging in drugs while we were playing happy hour, without a care in the world for what we kids were witnessing. We couldn't have cared less, though. We had front-row seats to all kinds of action in that club. I saw people get shot and stabbed. I saw hard-core pimping, with men slapping women upside their heads and taking their money— money they would dump on the table by the thousands—and putting hot hangers on their legs as punishment for not pulling it out their purses fast enough. Fights brewed in the corner and someone would yell out, "Get out the way, Little Wilson!" and I'd get out of the path of destruction just in the nick of time to see someone pouncing on another dude. I was in a place that was not appropriate for someone who was saved and sanctified and filled with the Holy Ghost. Or fifteen years old. There's even a picture floating around somewhere of me and a bunch of older men with guns sticking out of our pockets. Faking my toughness.

It didn't take long before our popularity started growing and the lies to our mothers started flying; I would say I was staying at a friend's house, my friends would say they were staying with someone else. We'd all pretend we had drum-major camp and just disappear for days at a time, playing gigs and getting paid. My mother bought that whole drum-major story line because my older brother was a drum major in high school and she too had been in the school marching band in high school. If anything, she was excited by the prospect of another son leading the band out there on the field. That made the "I've got to go to drum-major camp" excuse a really handy one to use to get out of the house for a few days. The only grown-up who knew what we were doing was a parent of one of the guys in the band; Mr. Thomas (not his real name) was cool with our being out, knowing that we'd be back sometimes as late as eleven at night. He would come out and chaperone us, talk to the club owner and make sure we got the money right. Of course, he couldn't watch all of us; there were seven or eight of us running around that club and inevitably, somebody—usually someone who didn't have kids—would slide me a drink. "Here, Little Wilson, taste this. It'll make you play better." By seven o'clock, we'd be finished playing, but soon, with our popularity rising, our happy hours show turned into happy nights and we wouldn't start until eight p.m. On Friday nights, we'd stay well after the sun finished its slow dance across the sky. I was the one too willing to push the boundaries. Everyone else's parents were telling them, "Don't do that or you'll die!" and I would respond cynically with a "Yeah right." Maybe I resented that the others had fathers who at least checked in.

That attitude didn't always play with the crowd. And occasionally, that mannish persona did get me into a world of trouble. On one particular night, it almost cost me my life. I was going with this older girl, which was quite the blessing, and, on this particular night when I left her sitting at the table to use the restroom, quite the curse. When I came back to the table, some dude, easily fifteen years my senior, was sitting there talking to her. In my seat. Now, I was standing there patiently, waiting for him to get up and stop talking to my girl, but he wouldn't budge. Rather, he leaned in a little closer and upped the level of game he was kicking to my lady. A real grown man would have told him to get up, but I stood there like an idiot, waiting, my body casting a shadow over the table while he stared into her eyes and made her giggle with whatever he was saying. Finally, I'd had enough.

"Man, get your ass out my seat," I said, my words shooting from my mouth like daggers.

That man looked at me and, without so much as a furrowed brow, turned his face back toward my girl and kept on talking. Talk about hot. I was undone! And I wasn't about to stand for it, either. "All right," I said, seething. "Be here when I get back."

I shot out of that club and ran on back to my mama's house and searched for the derringer pistol we had at home, hidden away. That metal, cold and hard and thick, was heavy in my palm but white-hot on my fingertips when I rushed back out the door, only to find my brother and his friends pulling into the driveway, hollering and screaming about how I needed to stay away from the club.

"Man, what's going on?" Ronnie demanded as he jumped out of his car. "There's talking in the parking lot over at the club about some guy figuring to kill my little brother, and now there's some old dudes down there waiting on you."

I was seventeen. The guy who had rallied the entire club to wait for me out in the parking lot was the daddy of one of my buddies—a prominent thirtysomething-year-old guy who had a store in Tulsa and who on this particular night had lowered himself down to the gutter to talk all kinds of mess about lighting me up. For once, I listened to my brother and stayed home that night, because sure as my name is Wilson, they were intent on taking me out. The next week, though, I went back there, that derringer in my pocket, ready for that grown man and his friends to pop off.

I didn't have to use it, though. Instead, I got an apology. "Hey, man," the guy said, "I was drunk and I didn't know that was you, Little Wilson. We were about to kill you."

I escaped death by the hands of the patrons that night, but there were other nights when it was my mother who was coming for my head. Before he got his own group, my brother was playing trumpet for this band called Magnificent Seven, and they were invited to play in some club in Kansas City, Missouri, from a Thursday to a Saturday—a weekend that he had to work. The Magnificent Seven bandleader was undeterred by my brother's work schedule: "The little Wilson plays horn, right?" he asked at one of his rehearsals. "Get him to play the horn parts." Initially, I asked my mother if I could go, and without hesitating, she said no. I wasn't about to turn that opportunity down, though, so when that bandleader's car left for KC, my horn and I were right there in the car with him. I disappeared for four days, to the utter horror and anger of my mother. She called my brother, begging him to find me, and, of course, he knew exactly where I was.

I didn't even see him coming. He walked right through that club door and grabbed me by the collar. "Boy, what you doing here?" he asked, fuming.

"I'm playing your parts," I said slyly.

Did I get in trouble for that one. And so many other escapades too numerous to mention. Finally, my father called and had a talk with my mom—told her, "Go on ahead and let the boy play. It ain't gonna hurt him. My nephew Lowell did it and he got popular at it. Maybe our boys will, too, if we let them go on ahead and try it for themselves." My mother didn't want to have any part of R & B and she definitely didn't want to see her sons playing it, either. It nearly killed her when our little brother, Robert, started to exhibit natural talent on the bass and beyond.

But finally, my mother came to understand that I was probably going to either lie about where I was or tell the truth and go play and sing somewhere anyway. So after a while, she had no other choice but to let me fly. Eventually, we came to an uneasy understanding about this thing. She didn't like it at all, but she wouldn't stop me, either. I didn't find out until I was much older that she used to cry every time I set foot out to play, especially when I traveled. I hate that I was the source of those tears. But I'm grateful that, as scared as she was about the kind of hold the music would have on me, she let me, Ronnie, and

Robert play our horns, strum our guitars, beat the drums, and sing our songs.

There was some healthy competition between my brothers and me, too. Tulsa has, for quite some time, been considered one of the top fifty largest urban areas in the United States, but my hometown was barely big enough for the Wilson boys. When we were teens, my brother Ronnie's band was popular around town; they'd play jazz and some popular tunes, but for a more mature set. What they didn't have was a singer like me. Their lead singer was Ray D. Rowe, a bluesman; he wrapped his powerful vocals around Bobby Blue Bland and Al Green, and I have to admit the ladies loved those songs. My band, by contrast, was playing Sly Stone and running around the stage with all this energy and dressing in fur boots with feathers hanging off and vests with fringe coming off of them and snatching up everybody for our funky ride. I started throwing Stevie Wonder and Donny Hathaway songs into the mix, as well as some Chicago and some Blood, Sweat and Tears and hipper songs that I knew the crowd would go crazy for because they were hit records. And sure enough, all of Tulsa was turning out to get worked up into a sweat-induced frenzy dancing, singing, and enjoying our music.

As word spread, Tulsans looking to hit the nightclubs started seeking out our band because we knew how to put on a show, which, of course impacted negatively on the number of people who showed up to hear my brother's band. This became glaringly obvious one night when Ronnie and his band finished playing a set to a near-empty club and caught sight of the parking lot at the club across the street, which was packed to the gills with cars and people squeezing into the front door. Anxious to see what the big deal was all about, Ronnie and his band left their club, hightailed it across the street, and pushed their way into the back of the packed club. "Who's that up on the stage?" my brother asked a fellow patron, craning his neck to see who had all of Tulsa grooving.

"Your little brother," somebody said.

"My little brother?" Ronnie shouted.

He was undone. My brother came right up to where we were playing; he and a couple of the guys from his band stood there with their arms folded across their chests, clearly upset and mean-mugging us while we played. Their anger only intensified when we finished our set with their break song. Yes, we stole that, too. Ronnie was smirking by the time I got off the stage.

"Man, does Mama know where you are?" he asked gruffly.

I didn't answer.

"You gotta get out of this club, Charles."

I was quick on the comeback: "No I don't," I answered firmly.

Ronnie stared me down for a beat, but he grudgingly understood that my love for music—a love that he shared—couldn't be quelled by a simple "don't do it." "Well then, you at least got to get out of this band and play in my band."

I categorically refused that demand, too. I liked playing in my own band. I liked my bandmates. I loved the sounds we were creating together. Ronnie and I argued for a little while longer before he and his band went on back to their empty club and I got back on the stage to entertain our packed house.

A few months later, Ronnie offered me fifty dollars to join his band. I told him I liked being the head of my own band. He upped the offer to seventy-five dollars, but I still refused. Then Ronnie stated it plain: "You're going to quit that band and join mine, and no, you don't have a choice."

My friends were all going off to college; everybody was going his or her separate way. I had no choice but to join his band, called Creative Sounds. I would play with them when I was home, and while I was in college at Langston University, I had another group I was in and out of, too, called the US Combo, one of the best bands I've ever been in in my life.

By sophomore year, though, I left school and headed back to my brother's band, which we named the Greenwood Archer Pine Street Band, after the main streets in our neighborhood in Tulsa. It was a clever homage to the Tulsa race riot of 1921, that catastrophic, racially motivated insurrection in which whites attacked blacks in their most prominent community, the Greenwood district, known back then as Black Wall Street. It was the wealthiest black community in the United States at the time, but it was obliterated in a matter of sixteen hours after blacks, anxious to protect a neighbor who'd been falsely accused of attacking a white woman, got into a deadly shoot-out with a legion of whites. By the time the smoke cleared, hundreds of blacks were injured, thousands of black Greenwood residents had been detained, 35 city blocks with 1,256 homes were destroyed by fire, some 10,000 blacks were left homeless, and anywhere from 39 to 300 people were killed, depending on whose count you trusted. As if this wasn't injustice enough, the events were long hidden from Tulsa and Oklahoma history, talked about only in quiet circles, if at all, with a hush so powerful all too many in our community either forbade each other to talk about it or forgot about it altogether. Not Ronnie, though. He knew what Greenwood, Archer, and Pine Streets stood for.

One hell of a tribute.

Later, when we tried but couldn't fit the entire band name on a flyer to promote a show, we shortened the Greenwood Archer Pine Street Band name into an acronym: The GAP Band. The nickname felt good. It stuck.

By then, our baby brother, Robert, who was terrifically talented at bass, was performing with us, too, and together, we took over the stages of clubs throughout Tulsa, playing anywhere there was music. We didn't care if it was a nightclub, a golf club, tennis courts, or a private party: if there was a need for a band, we were there. My mother never did get comfortable with the fact that all three of her sons were running around town performing secular music despite her protestations and warnings. Her thoughts on the matter meant something. But performing meant more.

Chapter 4

Get Up and Dance (Oops!)

My brothers and I were in rare form on this particular night—dressed up in cowboy gear and rhinestones and feathers and chaps we'd cut up and fringed out, shooting from song to song, using our white-hot energy to work the crowd into a frenzy that could have made a raucous Baptist tent revival look docile. That was where the funk led us. Sly and the Family Stone had paved a path like no other we'd seen before, mashing up colorful psychedelic bits of every musical genre we loved—gospel, soul, jazz, rock, even nursery rhymes—and smashing it into stages across the globe, and we had that spirit running through our veins, all up in our bones. We made it our personal mission to bring that vigor to the clubs in Tulsa, and our gigs were legendary: four thirty-to-forty-five-minute sets spread over five hours of pure, passionate musical adventure. And on this night, we were showing out. I was on the organ and sharing vocals with another band member; Ronnie was on trumpet, and because the bass player had bailed on us for some reason or another, we'd convinced my mother to let my little brother, Robert, who wasn't yet a permanent member, out of the house so he could play bass. Stevie Wonder, Donny Hathaway, Sly and the Family Stone, James Brown, rock music, folk with a soul edge, grooves we'd written for ourselves—all of it was laid out on that club stage.

Sometime before the dust settled, fellow Oklahoman and later-to-be Rock and Roll Hall of Famer Leon Russell, the keyboardist, songwriter, and sideman who was making a huge splash on the national scene with his version of the Tulsa Sound, came tumbling into the club with a bunch of drunk white guys. We were in rare form that night, playing grooves and rock and a fusion of rock and soul. I saw Leon and his boys sitting in the back—they were hard to miss. But none of us recognized who they were. We didn't leave until five in the morning and neither did they. The next weekend, we were there again and so were the white boys. But this time, they were sober. And when we played our set, they strolled backstage and had this guy, Buddy Jones, pass along a message: "Leon Russell wants to see you," he said. *The* Leon Russell. We were thrilled by the news and honored that our hometown's musical hero wanted to meet us. We didn't hesitate to invite him backstage. He got straight to the point: "I was here last weekend but I was drunk. I wanted to come back and see if what I heard was really real, or if I was drunk." We laughed easily, right along with him. "You guys are excellent," he said. "You want to go to the studio?"

A few weeks later, we were in the studio with one of the most famous singers to come out of Oklahoma, and a little while after that, we—my brothers, Ronnie and Robert, and I—were in the studio, working as Leon's backup band for recordings he did on his label, Shelter Records. We had a helluva time, too. Working with Leon opened up so many doors for us. Leon played the piano and had his rock-and-roll guitars attached to it, and we were playing the funkiest parts of his songs, so we had that rock-and-soul lick down. In the beginning, the relationship was mutually beneficial and extremely cool: Leon would pack the house; we went from playing to fifty people in a small club to performing in front of stadiums filled with fifty thousand screaming fans, which was huge for us, and Leon got a hot band that made his sets explosive. I would get up from the organ and skip across the stage, all of twenty years old, dressed up in capes with rhinestones and feathers all on my neck like Sly Stone, shouting like our father did from the pulpit on Sunday mornings, dancing and hopping and humping speakers—tearing the bottom off the whole show. Every time I jumped on the piano, I would break the microphone beneath the piano lid and they would have to go in there and put it back together again. I didn't care. I was just excited to be there, grateful for the chance to sing a song and dance for the people. The crowd would go wild.

When we weren't on the stage, we were having fun trying to write and learn together. Leon had his best friend, Buddy Jones, look out for The GAP Band, and Buddy ended up managing us. He had lyrics, too, so he played an integral part in helping us record our first album. He would write the lyrics and I would play at the piano, and magic would happen there. When we weren't creating, Buddy would feed my taste for stardom, sometimes even to his own detriment. Like that time I talked him into letting me drive Leon's Rolls-Royce all around downtown Tulsa. Without Leon's knowledge. "Stay on the south side," Buddy said, warning me, as he handed me the keys.

———

I got in that car and drove all over Tulsa, showing off in that Rolls as if I were paying the car note and buffing the hood on my own. I don't think there was a friend, foe, or stranger in sight who didn't see me in that ride, profiling. And then, wouldn't you know it, the damn thing broke down exactly where I wasn't supposed to be: on the north side of town. The oil pan blew a rod and the car just stopped on the side of the road, with me sitting behind the wheel, looking really stupid. I had to call Leon and tell him. I got into some serious trouble behind that one. Buddy, too. It was a pitiful sight watching the truck tow it off, with me standing there, wondering what Leon would do to me.

We got through that one, though, and, with Leon's help, we put out The GAP Band's album *Magicians Holiday*. I think maybe fifteen or sixteen people might have bought it, all of them either related to us or from our neighborhood in Tulsa. Today, I can understand why the album, the first we recorded as a band, didn't go anywhere; it was a piece for musicians that defied category. Honestly, we were caught between how to play and how to record. Leon was looking for us to be a black rock-anthem group with some funk and gospel all swirled in it, and we were busy trying to figure out something else. Do we stay funky? Do we stay gospel? Do we try to capture the magic we create onstage in the clubs? On that album, we were playing grooves like we were playing in front of a bunch of fans in the wee hours of an early Sunday: the songs were fifteen minutes long and we would take half of that getting to the bridge, just grooving on a tune that could have easily been broken up into three or four songs by the time the needle glided across the wax and to the end of the record. We didn't know how to put formats to grooves, how to make them radio-friendly fixtures. We didn't even understand what radio-friendly was: we were recording music for musically oriented people, not radio. So *Magicians Holiday* came from our heart, but it was a musician's record. Every record we cut until 1977 was a musician's record. We weren't ready for the airplay and that's why those early records didn't sell. Maybe a neighborhood or two in Oklahoma supported it, but we didn't become the superstars we intended to be off that record. Black people around our neighborhood didn't even know who Leon Russell was. We'd say, "We're recording with Leon Russell," and they'd say, "Leon Robinson? You're recording with him?" And we'd have to correct it over and over again.

Still, there were plenty of opportunities offered to us because of the musical sphere in which we danced, and we were taking full advantage of everything that came our way. When we weren't playing for Leon, we could open for anybody—and we did. Kansas. Kiss. We even opened for the Rolling Stones! We didn't have a record out that anybody knew, but a lot of rock groups had us open for them because they knew we had the experience and skills just by virtue of our association with Russell, and Buddy was hooking us up.

We got carried away one night, though, opening for the Rolling Stones. We were in Kansas City; there must have been forty to fifty thousand people, and when we went on, I got so into the music that we rolled right into "Jumpin' Jack Flash," at the time one of the biggest hits on the radio and one we routinely played during our sets. I don't want to sound like an idiot, but honestly, I didn't know it was their song. I was just showing out with a groove that we'd crank up anytime a rock guitar and a predominately white audience were involved. I was just intent on show-ing off. Eyes squeezed tight, the microphone pressed against my lips, the chanting crowd, my hands clapping like the hard-est rock-and-rollers in the game—all of that was my elixir. My fuel. I caught that feeling and I was gone. One minute I'd ask, "Should I jump off the stage and let them roll me around like a ball?" And then no sooner than I'd contemplated the downside of falling on my face, I'd be off to something else crazy, full of energy, and absolutely insane. Like singing "Jumpin' Jack Flash."

That was so disrespectful to a headliner, a fellow artist on a show, to perform his hit before he took the stage. But I wasn't thinking when I did it. I was so into the performance, so into the music, so in the moment, that I didn't notice. All I could see was that everybody in the audience was on their feet with their hands waving in the air, screaming and cheering. Mean-while, my brothers were trying to get my attention by changing the notes to try to lead me into singing something else. Finally, I realized what I'd done. The people backstage had to hold Mick Jagger back that night, he was so mad.

After that, there were no more shows with the Rolling Stones. Though our people were saying, "Put them on all the shows, they were incredible," the Stones' attorney and promoter were both shaking their heads furiously. "I don't think so!" they yelled. "If they're going to play the stars' hit record, they have no place on this tour!"

Eventually, that was Leon's sentiment, too. We would go out with him on his shows and go crazy on the stage and the next day, someone would show us the concert reviews with all this ink dedicated to saying that I was upstaging Leon and stealing his show. I didn't mean any harm; I was just excited. But Leon wasn't having it. We were scheduled to go to Africa with him, where he was going to be the only white artist performing, with James Brown and Aretha Franklin. Leon was blunt about it: "You're going to embarrass me," he said. What he really meant, I think, was that we were going to upstage him. I thought he wanted us to have a good time, but clearly, he didn't like that we were crushing the place. Had I known that, I would have toned it down. Instead, Leon and Buddy backed off after that. They let us go. And I thought our future was in jeopardy. I thought I'd ruined our chance to be stars.

When our touring with Leon ended and all the money we made out on the road was spent, we went back to being pretty regular guys with pretty regular jobs. I was working for some computer company, Ronnie was working for a pharmacy, and Robert didn't have a job, and, as a result, was losing his car, his refrigerator, and other material assets. We needed money. More important, we needed to earn it by doing what sustained our souls *and* by having a manager who could secure us a record deal and get us working again.

We thought we'd found that in Mace Neufeld. Today, Mace is known for his legendary career as one of Hollywood's most prestigious producers, with feature films stretching from *The Frisco Kid* and *No Way Out* to four film adaptations of Tom Clancy novels (*The Hunt for Red October, Patriot Games, Clear and Present Danger,* and *The Sum of All Fears*) and, more recently, the Clint Eastwood–directed *Invictus,* starring Morgan Freeman. But back in the sixties and early seventies, through his firm BNB Management, he was a budding songwriter who helped pioneer personal management for some of the music industry's heavyweights, including the Carpenters, Randy Newman, Herb Alpert, and Jim Croce. When he got ahold of The GAP Band, he saw the vision and set about helping us secure a record deal with RCA, under its Tattoo Records label. The entire band moved to California to be close to him while he and his partners produced our music; there, we recorded our second album, *The GAP Band*, and released two singles off of it— "Out of the Blue (Can You Feel It)" and "Little Bit of Love." We thought we were on our way to the win with that album, but, like *Magicians Holiday*, it floundered, with sales that went nowhere and barely a showing on the charts. With my brothers and I now leading a band nine members deep, we were struggling—both professionally and personally.

There was a lady out there in California, Harriette Jones (not her real name), who tried her best to help us while we tried hard to find our way. She kept us for a good year, for which I will always be grateful. She had a two-bedroom apartment and four kids of her own; still, she let me, my brothers, and our roadies—we didn't have a nickel in our pockets, mind you, but we had roadies!—sleep in her place. I had gone to school with some of her kids, so she knew us, but more important, she believed in us. There were fourteen people in this house, including her four children, and Miss Jones fed us for a solid year, asking for nothing in return.

We almost got that poor lady kicked out of her place. The manager saw a lot of people going in and out of the apartment, but he didn't have a clue that we were all living in there until about six months in. He told Miss Jones he wanted us out. So I suggested we butter him up. It was soon to be his birthday, and I thought it would be a great idea to play a birthday concert for him by the pool. Who could deny us when we performed especially for him? We dragged all this equipment to the side of the pool and set up like we were about to play the Garden. We were ready to win this guy over!

When the landlord got back, the whole building was down there, partying and drinking and splashing in that pool, prepping for what we intended to be the birthday party of all birthday parties. And when he walked in, the whole place went nuts, yelling, "Surprise!" On cue, we went in, putting it down like The GAP Band was wont to do, with all of the funk we could muster in our bodies and fingers and voices and instruments. But as soon as we hit those first few notes, the whole plan backfired: we blew out the fuse to the whole building! That landlord turned all kinds of red and damn near went crazy on us; you could practically see the steam rising from the top of his head. "Get them out of here! Get them out of here now!" he demanded. "Right now!"

While we were struggling to hold on to our sleeping quarters on Miss Jones's apartment floor, The GAP Band was trying desperately to stay together, and Mace wasn't helping the effort. Indeed, Mace and his partners were trying to break us up. "Listen," he said one afternoon after summoning me to their Beverly Hills office. "They don't want the brothers; they just want Charlie Wilson."

The record company that made the offer had this grand idea that I would be the black Elton John, that they would sit me behind a piano and give me gorgeous music with infectious lyrics to sing and let the world hear me stripped down—sans the guitars; sans the bass and heavy drums; sans the funk; sans the big band and the rhinestones, cowboy hats, and psychedelic colors; sans the funk; sans my brothers—and shine the spotlight down on only me. Elton John had hits to his credit and they were convinced that with the right music and grooming, I could get in there and beat him. They had writers lined up and they had a check ready. The offer: one million dollars.

"Oh man," I said, alternately excited and pissed. "Why you trying to break up my family?"

"No disrespect, Charles, to your family," Mace said. "We just see a really big picture here by yourself and we think you could be bigger than Elton John."

Though it was meant to flatter me, instead that offer landed me in a funk. After all, I was just a guy happy to be performing on a stage where I could see my brothers and love them up close, happy that we were on this journey together. In my heart, my biggest dream was to be famous, and what progress I had made toward that goal I'd achieved with my brothers. I couldn't leave them behind.

"If you can't take my brothers, then you can't have Charlie Wilson," I said.

Every once in a while I consider what my brothers would have done had they been presented with the same proposition. I suspect they would have left my ass. In a heartbeat. I wasn't considering the big picture back then. I was just thinking about my brothers, as I did our whole career. There are times when I think about what a million dollars meant back then and how desperately I could have used it in the hard times ahead, but who knows what would have happened had I not stayed. Maybe if I was out there on the road alone, without my brothers and addicted, I would have died.

. . .

After that emotionally dramatic episode, Mace and his partners dropped us and disappeared. I don't think it was just because I refused to go solo; I think they couldn't figure out how to manage us. The GAP Band had three different heads, with three different attitudes and three different vibes, and management was looking at us and thinking, "This is going to be a mess trying to manage all three of the brothers. If we can't have Charlie by himself, we'll back out." Losing management again felt like death.

But Miss Jones refused to give up hope that we could make it and helped us set up a showcase in a local auditorium, where she invited Dick Griffey and Don Cornelius, who had just started the SOLAR record label and were making a splash with Shalamar, the group they'd curated from the dance floor of their iconic show, *Soul Train*. All the guys from the band worked hard to fill that entire audience so that auditorium would be hyped when we took the stage to wow Dick and Don. When the time came, all the neighborhood kids showed up and showed out for The GAP Band. We were up there going hard, too, pulling out all our best grooves and rocking out with that trademark energy we brought to every gig we played. The audience was into it, but the organizers were off to the side, trying to tell us what to play. "Y'all don't know no James Brown? You can't play Stevie Wonder or some Top Forty or something?" they asked. I thought we were doing just fine, and our drummer at the time, Calhoun, a white boy, helped turn up the crowd when he came from behind his drum set and got on the mic to put his stamp on some popular soul songs. We definitely won the crowd over with that. But man, I couldn't take my eyes off the two empty seats we'd reserved for the two people we wanted most to be there. Dick and Don never showed.

We didn't give up. Yet another manager linked us up with Joe Green, a background singer who'd worked with and was very close to Quincy Jones. He offered to make the introduction to the legendary producer—one of my all-time heroes. Joe hooked us up with A&M Records and helped us record two singles intended to capture Quincy's attention: "Hard Time Charlie" and "This Place Called Heaven." But neither of the songs went anywhere. Plus, Quincy was preoccupied putting in work with the funk group the Brothers Johnson ("Strawberry Letter 23," "Stomp") and Leon Ware, the powerhouse songwriter and composer who penned hit songs for the Jacksons ("Got to Be There"), the Isley Brothers, Minnie Riperton ("Inside My Love"), and Donny Hathaway, as well as the entirety of Marvin Gaye's album *I Want You*, and Quincy just didn't have the time or inclination to add The GAP Band to the mix. Back then I was hurt by that because I knew intuitively that Quincy could take us somewhere special.

Soon after that, we all headed back to Oklahoma. We simply couldn't sustain ourselves out in California, not with that many band members and no real game plan for how we'd get new management and another record deal.

It didn't take long for me to feel that itch again—to feel that burning desire to head back to California and make something happen for us. So I called a meeting with the guys and said, "I'm going back to California. Who's with me?" The other guys in the group were settling into steady gigs and didn't want to disturb that groove, and my brothers were leery about the move, too.

"This music business is too confusing and we don't want to be eating cold cereal with water instead of milk and sleeping on people's floors anymore," they said.

I understood fully the implications. So I said, "I'll quit my job and go get something for us, and when I do, I'm coming back for my brothers."

And that's what I did. I was back in California just a few months after that, dead set on scoring something more secure for my brothers and me. A record deal maybe. Or at least someone who could help us get one and, perhaps, manage our affairs.

That's when I met Lonnie Simmons. I'd gone to a nightclub he owned out in Los Angeles, called the Total Experience. D. J. Rogers ("Say You Love Me," "Givin' It Up Is Givin' Up,"), whom I knew from our days together at Shelter Records with Leon, was performing there, and when I saw him up on that stage, it was a sight for sore eyes. My brothers and I had gotten to know him when he came to the Shelter offices in Tulsa to record. We met him at the studio whenever he was in town and became fast friends. He'd come by my house and I'd go kick it with him back at his hotel, and if he was performing, we'd fill in as his band. So when D. J. saw me walking through the Total Experience, he went crazy. It was great to see him, too.

Just as I'd settled in to check out his rehearsal set, D. J. had a moment on the stage. He was having problems with his band; they couldn't get it right while they were practicing, so much so that D. J. went off on them. Right there in front of me, he turned to his band and said, "I'm going to say it one more time: if you miss this cue, I'm firing everybody in this band." They missed that cue.

"Everybody get out of my face," he yelled. "You're fired!"

Maybe he was truly annoyed with his band's inability to get the sound he was looking for, but I think that what he really wanted was to hire The GAP Band. "Where are your brothers, Charlie?" he asked.

"At home," I said.

"Can you get them here by tomorrow?" he asked.

"As long as you're paying," I said easily.

He flew my brothers in the next day, and we played for D. J. for a while at the Total Experience. Now, this was an entirely different kind of energy from what we were used to in the clubs back in Tulsa; this was Los Angeles and that club was banging! Every night, it was teeming with glitterati—jam-packed lines around the corner, bottles popping, beautiful women everywhere, the hottest music pumping from the speakers, and stars galore on the stage. And everybody, it seemed, wanted a piece of that action. I was backstage one evening when I overheard one of the members of the Dramatics saying, "Man, I should get Lonnie to rep us."

I said to myself: "Wow, now, that's a smooth idea."

Then came the night when Lonnie heard me sing "You Can Always Count on Me." He said the magic words: "Man, I love your voice," he told me as I sat at the piano. "You should let me manage you. We could get rich."

Lonnie was managing D. J. already and had helped to secure

him a deal with RCA, so I trusted that he had some connections and was capable of making a few things happen for us. He drove around in a Rolls-Royce and the fast money was flowing every which way. I was convinced that he would be able to shift our career into gear quickly. I knew we could cut a better record than the one he'd helped D. J. to produce; I just needed him to put us on.

We danced around the partnership for quite a few weeks. He'd say he was drawing up a contract, but one never materialized. In the interim, he'd try to offer us work. I insisted we couldn't work together until there was an actual contract to sign. When he finally presented papers, I was hesitant. "What kind of contract is that?" I asked. It was an honest question; I'd never really read a contract before and I didn't understand any of the terms.

"Don't worry about that. You just sing, I'll handle the business, and me and you are gonna get rich," he said insistently.

That's how we ended up with Lonnie in our corner. Initially in our working relationship and in our personal regard for one another, Lonnie, my brothers, and I became family— so close that my brother Robert even called Lonnie "Dad." He gave great advice—both professionally and personally—and we trusted him completely, so much so that we offered to make him a fourth member of The GAP Band. We thought nothing of involving him in every aspect of what we were doing, from allowing him to put his name on the songs we wrote to giving him credit for publishing and producing. Chalk that up to inexperience, naïveté, and our starry-eyed investment in the Total Experience, a ride that would take The GAP Band to its highest of highs and, eventually, its lowest of lows.

Chapter 5

Party Train

Back in the day, the best music managers found the talent and made the way and practiced a no-holds-barred vocation when it came to their clients: they bargained with record companies, wrestled tour promoters, orchestrated deals that guaranteed their artists' great-grandchildren would live a life of leisure if they so chose. Sometimes the manager's work came with quite the reputation—threats, intimidation, violence. It happened. But when there was magic, the superstars won.

Still, the American musical landscape is littered with artists who danced in the spotlight and made their mark as pop cultural icons, only to crash and burn, undone by their managers. The lies. The bogus bookkeeping. The convoluted contracts that keep artists indebted into perpetuity. In some cases, those managers were outright monsters—using the threats, intimidation, and violence against the very people they were charged with advocating for and protecting, all while lining their pockets with their artists' hard-earned cash. I wanted to avoid that kind of manager.

To be honest, at first we were just happy to have a manager. The GAP Band had already had a series of recording deals that went nowhere, and this guy set about promising us the stars, the moon, and all of the sky that embraced them. It was Lonnie who got us our seminal deal with Mercury Records; he set up the audition with Charlie Fach, then the vice president of artists and repertoire at the iconic label, home to acts such as the Bar-Kays, Parliament, Con Funk Shun, Kurtis Blow, and Kiss. Singing for Charlie that day was an easy thing to do: all that was required of me was to sit at that piano and sing my song. I chose "You Can Always Count on Me," the single from *Magicians Holiday* that had wowed Lonnie when we first met at the Total Experience. With a laser-sharp focus and the clarity of a man determined, I sat down at that piano, put my fingers on those black and white keys, closed my eyes, and sang my song with the might of angels. When I took my last breath, hit that final note, and opened my eyes, there was Charlie, staring at me slack-jawed. "Where," he said breathlessly, "did you learn how to sing like *that*?"

"My parents," I said without hesitation.

Lonnie, anxious to seal the deal, asked me to step outside so that he could talk to the Mercury Records executive privately, a request I honored without hesitation. He came back out with a signed contract sealing a partnership between The GAP Band and the label, a step forward that meant my brothers and I were well on our way to getting exactly what Lonnie promised we'd have: fame and fortune.

From the outside looking in, it did look like we had that, too: though our first single off our 1979 album *The GAP Band*, "Baby Baba Boogie," fell flat—it was an ill-advised attempt to enter the musical big leagues by riding the wave of the disco craze—we hit the radio waves hard with our second single, "Shake," which climbed to number four on the *Billboard* R & B chart and, later, our slow groove "I'm in Love." All we wanted to do was hear our music on the radio and get paid, but the latter was slow in coming. When "Shake" took off, we believed Lonnie when he said it didn't produce the kind of money required to change our lives financially. "I ain't quite got it yet," he'd say. "I just have to work with it a little different, make the next single go bigger."

And so we left the business end of things to him while we worked hard to come up with more hits. We were on the stage practically every night, connecting and vibing with our fans and recording the exchanges between us and our audience so that we could really get our fingers on the pulse of what was hitting for both us and them. Then we'd put in studio overtime in the daytime, listening to cassette tapes of our performances and finding the grooves that resonated with who we were as a band and the fans who loved our music. There was magic in those exchanges, and they were a literal gold mine for the advancing of our art. Indeed, that's where we found the groove to "I Don't Believe You Want to Get Up and Dance (Oops!)." We were performing in Pittsburgh and the crowd was chanting and singing while my little brother was crisscrossing the stage, sweating and furrowing his brow and tossing his head back while he laid into a particularly boisterous solo on his bass. When we got to the studio the next day and played back the tape, we heard the audience and were inspired. "Oops" went on to climb to number four on the *Billboard* charts, and *The GAP Band II*, buoyed by our foray into the hard funk grooves we'd started to become known for in our stage performances, went gold, selling more than five hundred thousand copies, climbing to number three on the *Billboard* R & B chart and number forty-two on the Pop chart. "Steppin' (Out)," "Party Lights," and "Oops" established us as powerhouses in the industry—made people fall in love with us in a way that we'd always wanted but had never realized.

Still, there was no money. We were out on the road, touring and packing in huge audiences at large venues with thousands of screaming fans, and spending practically every other waking moment in the studio, churning out hits, yet Lonnie insisted that by the time he paid all our expenses—the tour buses, roadies, hotels, travel, studio time, and the like—there was almost nothing left over for us. He repeated that same, tired story when *The GAP Band III*, with our monster hits "Yearning for Your Love," "Burn Rubber," and "Humpin'," crashed the charts and funked its way straight into the radios, dance floors, and hearts of our fans.

The truth is, while The GAP Band was paving the way for modern-day hip-hop and R & B with our flashy onstage antics and high-energy performances, we released nine albums and were still broke, as incredible as that may seem. We would go out on the road and then come off after what we thought was a hugely successful tour and Lonnie would say we owed *him* three million dollars. My brothers and I would sell out coliseums, yet when the show was over and I'd given the audience all I had, I found myself with barely a penny to my name. I would sit in the corner and cry. Lonnie seemed unmoved. There were many nights that he would simply toss a one-hundred-twenty-five-dollar per diem our way and keep it moving, leaving us with barely enough to buy food, to say nothing of new clothes and the like. I would wear hand-me-downs when I was offstage and then go onstage with these outrageous outfits tailored just for me. I'd shine there. But behind the scenes, I was a wreck, as were my brothers. I was broke and incredibly unhappy, and my growing despair was compounded by my rapidly growing addiction to alcohol and drugs, which made us easy prey.

And when we would ask why we had so little money or why his name was on the songs that we wrote, Lonnie would push back. This certainly happened one night when we were at the Total Experience studios and he was going on and on about how hard he was working on our behalf but saying that he was still having a tough time putting money in our pockets. I'm no mathematician, but none of it was adding up. The record company gave us a budget for videos and promotion and things like that, and we recorded in the Total Experience studios, so studio time was free. It simply didn't seem as if we were spending enough money to justify having barely anything left over after touring. It was even more frustrating to realize that while we were walking around in rags, Lonnie was experiencing what looked like an embarrassment of riches. He was driving Rolls-Royce and Bentley cars all around town, and he had all these slick, impeccably tailored suits with pockets that seemed to me to be full of cash. He tried, too, to hide it from us, going so far as to drive the older-model Rolls he had when we first met him whenever he knew we'd be around. I called him on that one particular night after seeing him on the other side of town in a sharp new ride I knew had set him back close to one hundred thousand dollars.

"You know," I told him, "you keep saying there's no money, but I just saw you driving a ragtop, dark blue Bentley," I said casually as we sat in the studio. I'd barely gotten the words out of my mouth before he was in my face, his breath and spittle hot on my cheek, the fire in his eyes burning a hole through mine.

"So what?" Lonnie barked back, his eyes narrowed like slits.

The more belligerent he got, the louder our argument grew, and the room, full of people who worked at the Total Experience, got thick with tension. And then, before I saw it coming, Lonnie came at me.

I was yelling, "You ain't gave me shit! Nothing! You're the only one rich, and here you are, talking about we still owe you money!" I reared back and hawked a glob of spit in his face before the fellas in the room separated the two of us, holding us back while we screamed at each other. "Where's my money?" I demanded. "If me and you started this, where is my part?

"Let me go!" I yelled at the dude restraining me, shaking myself from his grip. "I ain't never, ever coming back here!"

I was so upset. *So very upset.* I couldn't tell you how I made it back to my home in Westlake, between the tears of anger and the throbbing headache and the sheer disbelief that Lonnie had come for me the way he did. But before I could settle in, there was a knock at my door. Convinced it was Lonnie or one of his boys there to hurt me, I grabbed my sawed-off shotgun and stood my ground on the side of the entrance to my home. "I'm not opening up this door!" I yelled, cocking the hammer and aiming my shotgun, my finger on the trigger. Somebody was going to die that night, but it was not going to be me.

"Man, let me in, I just want to talk to you," the man at the door said. I recognized his voice from the record label, so I let him and his companion inside.

"Lonnie is back at the office going crazy," one guy said. "As soon as you left, everybody was like, 'Dude, what's wrong with you? Do you know what you just did? He makes it so all of us can eat! You beat up the guy making all the millions of dollars.'"

"Millions?" I'm thinking.

The other guy chimed in: "He was going crazy, talking about, 'I don't know what happened. Where'd he go? I have to talk to him. Somebody go say something to him.'" He got quiet for a second, and then he said something that unmoored me, left me undone. "Man, if I were you, I'd ask for three million dollars to go back. Nothing less."

I wish I had taken that advice. Instead, I kept what happened that night to myself. I didn't tell my brothers. I didn't confront Lonnie. All I could see in front of me was the imminent demise of our careers, and the only thing I could concern myself with was how to keep our band from falling to pieces. I wanted us to keep recording. I needed us to. Because at the very least, if we were not recording and performing, surely, we were going to go back to having nothing. To being nobody.

. . .

My self-esteem was so shattered, I couldn't even see that I might have been in a position to obtain at least a portion of what was due to me and my family. You have to understand: con-flict—pushing back—was never, ever part of my nature. I had a passive-aggressive personality and had developed an acute case of low self-esteem. Asserting myself, showing my true feelings, was never, ever my way. If I didn't like something, I would keep it to myself—hold it in until it piled up like stinking, putrid garbage, festering and overflowing, until, finally, I couldn't stand the smell of it any longer and exploded. But it took me a long time to detonate. And when I finally did, it would be internally directed, hardly ever externally so. Instead, I concerned myself with making sure others' feelings didn't get hurt, as if their emotional states were more important than my own. This, coupled with my propensity to trust anyone who crossed my path, made it easy for people to take advantage of me. They would see this nice guy whose sole mission was to please, and they would zero right in on that, mistake it for weakness, and run with it. It was this insecurity that Rick James picked up on one night in the club, as I described in the prologue. I wish I could have used some of that Rick James hubris to protect my brothers and me, but my timidity made it easy for Total Experience to have its way with us—with our talent, our fame, and, finally, with our money.

Here I was, Charlie Wilson from The GAP Band, traveling the world, and I couldn't even buy myself simple things. Like my own ride, though that finally changed when I walked into a Mercedes-Benz dealership one day just to see what was on the floor, and the salesman gave me a crazy look and told me not to touch the cars, as if I were some bum off the street or something. And how could I counter it? I didn't have any money. I *was* broke—living off pennies and someone else's good credit. I looked just a step above a loiterer, I'm sure. I got so angry at the salesman and at myself and the financial wall I was up against that I stormed out of the showroom and out to a pay phone on the street. Pushed to my edge, I called the Total Experience offices and told whoever answered the phone that I was going to break everything in that dealership—every window, every desk, every car, everything I could lay my hands on—unless someone came down there right that instant and bought me a car. They were down there in fifteen minutes with everything they needed to put the keys in my hand.

It took a second tantrum for me to get the money I needed to do something nice for my mother. I wanted desperately to give back to the woman who gave me life, not just because she was my mother but also because back in Tulsa, she was facing off against a lot of jealousy and envy from "friends" who gave her a hard time because she had three famous sons and it looked like we weren't taking care of her. That much was the truth. We loved and cared deeply about her, of course, but that love and care sure couldn't be measured in material goods. So just one time, I wanted to do something nice for my mother, and I had to get loud and in someone's face to make that happen. That outburst yielded me thirty thousand dollars—which I promptly gave to my mother as a Christmas present. That is the only time I remember ever getting any kind of substantial cash during my days performing on the Total Experience label. All that fame, no fortune.

Soon enough, all of that abuse my brothers and I suffered at the hands of Total Experience started eating away at our relationship with each other. We were tight and we loved to write and make music together, and there were happy times in that. But after we got really successful, around *The GAP Band III*, when "Yearning for Your Love" and "Burn Rubber" were hitting, we all started looking up and saying, "Okay, we haven't made any money," and pointing fingers as to whose fault that was, and that sentiment only got worse when *The GAP Band IV* dropped. We were miserable, and, soon enough, Ronnie, Robert, and I were taking out our frustrations on each other. We'd fallen so far apart that we barely spoke to one another.

Be clear: I always wanted to be protective of my brothers and believe they felt the same way about me. All three of us wanted to be democratic about everything, to have an equal say in it all. But it wasn't always easy to pull off, particularly as we got more popular and still had no money. We never really appointed anyone "the boss"—the person who would be responsible for making the decisions and taking the lead and being the mouthpiece for our unified front. One of us should have stood tall and said, "I'm the boss and this is how we're going to do it, and here is the plan for how to get it done." We didn't do that. Instead, we each assumed, without ever talking about it, that one of the others was going to do it. Still, people all over the world would say, "Charlie is the leader of The GAP Band," and that would cause tension. Yet as the years went by, my brothers stopped doing things to make sure they had a public face in our group. Everybody stopped going to interviews except for me. I was the one getting up early and doing the promos, while they said they had headaches and backaches and couldn't go. Eventually, when people, the press included, saw the three of us together, they only wanted to talk to Charlie. My brothers got angry about it. Our bond started to fray.

· · ·

I gave everything I had to The GAP Band—all of us did—but as long as the business wasn't right and we weren't seeing any money, as long as we were being taken advantage of and feeling as if we were stuck in some mess that we just couldn't see our way out of, we were broken. And there was no fixing us. Drugs took the edge off, provided solace.

Chapter 6

My Years of Living Dangerously

It has been twenty years since I felt the hot glass of a crack pipe against my lips and the burn of cheap vodka slow-snaking its way across my tongue—two decades since I tasted the bitterness of cocaine dripping from my nasal passages and down the back of my throat, all of them numbed from the blast of the powder. Today, I am clean. Right now, at this very moment, I am sober. Yet I'm clear that I am an addict whose recovery continues and always will be a work in progress, wholly dependent on three specific commitments: to stay away from drugs, to surround myself with people who do the same, and to employ the kind of strength that comes only when one surrenders himself to something more powerful than us all.

Still, the truth of the matter is this: a relapse is as close to me as the distance between my hand and my nostrils.

Today—this very minute—is all I have.

It is all I can depend on.

I was about fourteen when I had my first taste—right around the time my father left our family and I started performing with my friends at A Blue Monday, the after-hours club we played that drew in crowds of adults who taught at our school during the day but at night morphed into hot-blooded club-goers who smoked, drank, and danced suggestively, doing what grown-ups do when the kids aren't watching. At the club, we'd talk casually to one another and I was even on a first-name basis with them. But when I got back to school, I'd have to call them Mr. or Mrs. So-and-So. Sometimes I would slip and call Mr. Parker, the school principal, Pookie, the nickname he went by at the club, where he hung out. A lot. One time, Mr. Parker and I actually got into it in the school hallway when he confronted me about calling him Pookie after he played me by putting drinks on my tab at A Blue Monday. When I saw him in the hallway, I said, "Pookie, man, you owe me fifteen dollars. You put drinks on my tab, so you cost me money!" I wasn't drinking yet, so I didn't even know what a tab was. But I was out fifteen dollars that night. I got expelled for about thirty minutes. Let's just say that he was reminding me to call him Mr. Parker while on school premises, especially in a hallway full of students. But I was full of myself back then. I was a boy in a grown-up world, and it wasn't long before I was doing what grown-ups do.

Initially, I started drinking. We were making about twelve to fourteen dollars apiece per night, and all the adults who showed up to listen were sitting at the bar doing exactly what Pookie did: putting their drinks on my tab. They would drink up twenty dollars' worth of liquor and at the end of the night, not only would I not have any money coming to me, I'd actually owe the club cash for all the drinks flowing onto my "tab." So to keep watch over it and socialize with the people who were coming out to see our band every week, I started sitting at the bar between sets, charging my own drinks to my own tab and sipping and laughing with the high school teachers and newly graduated college students who hung out at the club.

Then came the night when I stumbled on a guy snorting cocaine in the club bathroom. It was the first time I'd ever seen drugs, let alone seen someone using them, and, honestly, it scared me. He had it all lined up on the sink counter and he was snorting it. I assumed it was LSD, which was all anybody talked about back in those days, you know—that "acid" that made you hallucinate, made you trip. I can still hear my mother warning all of us to stay away from it: "Boy, that LSD will kill you! Stay away from dope!" she'd say, shaking her finger. So to me, the most dangerous thing in the world was LSD; I didn't want any part of it and that was that. But this guy in the bathroom, he was talking about something different.

"This is coke," he said to me before leaning in to snort another line. "Want some?"

"No, that's okay," I said, quickly making my way out of the bathroom.

Still, I watched him when he came out—I saw him from my perch up on the stage. And he wasn't acting any kind of way; he was dancing and behaving normally, having himself a good time; he wasn't running around, trying to climb up the wall or pretending he had bat wings and could fly up to the ceiling and hang upside down. He looked no different from anyone else there, having a few drinks, enjoying the music, mixing it up with friends and romantic interests. He looked cool.

I wanted some of that. Some of that cool.

So when I saw him heading back into the bathroom, I went in there behind him. "Hey, man, um, let me try a little of that," I said as easily as I could manage to.

"What? You want some of what I'm flying on?" he asked as he spread and chopped some new lines of coke on the bathroom counter. "Come on and get you a little taste."

I took a snort—just a little into my nose, copying what I'd seen the guy do earlier. It stung the inside of my nasal passage and made me cough something fierce. But it smoothed out my edges almost instantly—it relaxed me a little bit. And I kind of liked it. I didn't do any more coke that night or for a long time after that, but I remembered that feeling.

You never forget the first time.

That's the way it is. It seems like the coolest thing ever to do drugs because it makes you feel ten feet tall. You tell yourself that this one time will be the last time, until the next time comes and you do it again. In the worlds I began traveling, everyone else was doing it. I didn't want to feel left out. I wanted to feel bigger, stronger, better—more in control.

Thing is, some people are strong enough to snort, smoke, or pour a little liquor for themselves and move on. But the ones with addictive tendencies get stuck. Like I did. I put that poison into my body and it robbed me of everything I had: my livelihood, the family and friends who truly loved me, my sanity. My dignity. Cocaine, crack, and liquor were a collective shotgun to my head, and every moment of the day, I thought I would die unless I took those drugs. That's the way addiction works. "It" makes you do drugs. Not somebody else. "It." And "It" has no mercy—doesn't care if you're a sinner or a preacher, a mother or a motherless child, a boy or an old, dirty man, if you're an executive of a Fortune 500 company or pulling minimum-wage double shifts at the local discount store, if you graduated from an expensive university or earned a degree in hard knocks on the hardest block in the hood. "It" is a demon, and once you start with it, it will take you out—rob you of everything you've ever loved and destroy anything you've ever thought of having. "It" will make you wholly irrational. I should know. I experienced it firsthand. Drug dealers didn't make me do it. My friends didn't make me do it. "It" was making me do it.

"It" had me.

I was powerless against drugs. I was self-medicating to numb the pain and feelings of anger and inadequacy that had all but consumed me, even when the world thought I was at the top of my game. I was the lead singer of The GAP Band, yet, in reality, I was penniless and at odds with my brothers. I was no longer that confident boy in the club but an insecure man worried about money and family.

My descent into addiction was gradual. My drug use was recreational and occasional when I was a young teen, but by the time I started taking drugs regularly, I was young, fresh, and excited about being Charlie Wilson from The GAP Band. Doing drugs is what stars did. As clichéd as it might sound, snorting and smoking and drinking were simply a part of the business— part of life as a celebrity, certainly in the seventies and eighties, when the drug culture, dusty and battered by the cultlike atmosphere of the hippie/flower-child movement of the sixties, got spit-shined by the glamour and star power of the funk and disco eras. When we wrote songs, we partied. When we recorded, we partied. When we were on tour, running from venue to venue, we partied. When we were in our dressing rooms, waiting to kill the stage, we partied. And when we played, we partied harder. Everywhere I went, I rode shotgun on a wave of drugs and alcohol that gave me the courage to create, perform, and move in a crowd that had more stars than a Tulsa late-night summer sky.

Taking the drugs never made me feel better about myself—never gave me the courage or bravado I craved. All it did was make me shrink deeper into a depression, deeper into a darkness full of fear that I could neither measure up to what my fans thought I was (successful, paid) nor attain what my entertainment peers had (Grammy Awards, money, beautiful homes and cars, access). I went from a confident teen to a gutted, insecure man.

Rather than feel hurt or attempt to fix the problem, I chose to be both angry about my circumstances and numb to reality. And my addiction made that easy to do. It also made me a really nasty guy, particularly when it came to women. All the tough behavior I witnessed between my parents—the arguments, the womanizing, my father leaving and virtually disappearing from our lives—I mimicked and inflicted on all the people I claimed I loved. I did not know how to have a healthy, positive, sustainable relationship with a woman. I had a string of failed relationships dating back to high school, when I was drinking and having sex with abandon. My first daughter was the product of one such affair. Later, when I was riding high on my celebrity with The GAP Band, and groupies were everywhere and my drug and alcohol addiction was full-blown, I met a woman who eventually became my live-in girlfriend. She and I had a child together—my second daughter—but that relationship, too, was doomed to failure. I was always paranoid—always accusing her of whatever dark thoughts I had on my mind. It was horrible. I was horrible.

What's worse is my children saw it all. I loved my children with all of my being, but my dependence on drugs and alcohol created so much havoc that there came a time when their mothers wouldn't let me see them. My older daughter was in Oklahoma with her mother, and she remembers her grandparents and mother laying down the law and saying, "You can't go visit your daddy." Even more hurtful, on the few occasions when their mothers would allow visits, my kids, who thought I was rich because they were hearing me on the radio and seeing me on television doing shows such as *Soul Train* and *American Bandstand*, would, upon sight, ask me for money. Before they could push out even a simple "Hi," they had their hands out. I wasn't annoyed by their requests; I was crushed that I didn't have the means to give it. As a father charged with caring for his family, this was difficult to reconcile. It took some hard work for my children and me to mend our relationship after all of that trauma, but I am grateful we fixed it and moved on to loving one another in much healthier ways.

My daughters weren't the only ones living under the impression that I was rich back then. One day that perception almost cost me my life. I was prey. I had traveled back to Oklahoma with all this money in my pocket—cash that I'd earned from producing a song or two for Pebbles, an R & B singer who later went on to manage TLC. The first thing I did was take it back to Tulsa so that I could share it with my mother, sister, and children, both of whom were by then living there with their mothers. It was Christmastime, and all I wanted to do was make it nice for them. But I'm not going to lie: I wanted, too, to flash some of that cash around because that made me feel bigger—made me feel, for once, like a star. I'd never had that much money at one time. So I walked all around town with that money in my pocket like a damn fool, though everyone who loved me warned me to put it away.

I refused. Instead, I'd pull it out of my pocket and show it off to anyone who dared to look while I was riding around Tulsa with two guys I knew, one of whom I trusted because he used to be my drummer back in the early days of my career. I was sitting in the front seat of his car, counting out hundreds and bragging about my big bank, and he kept saying, "Man, you better stop running around with that money, Charlie. Somebody is going to get you." And somebody did. That "friend" had a few rental homes around Tulsa and while we were out, he convinced me that an old friend wanted to see me and that I should let him drop me off over there to check him out. So this guy runs me by one of his houses and tells me to go inside. Like a fool, I do it. And what was waiting for me on the other side of that door?

A man in a ski mask with a gun in his hand.

This man laid me on the floor and took all my money. Every penny. To make it worse, he actually put that gun to my head and told me to "sing a little something." Today, I can laugh about that—truly, it's the funniest thing. But when it was happening, I was shaking, sure that I was going to die that day. I did what this man told me to do and I sang. I don't know what words came out of my mouth or how it sounded, but I sang for my life. And when I was done, he let me up and let me on out of that house.

Now, you would think that I would get to the other side of that door and run down those stairs thankful for my life. But when I got onto that porch, my addiction—the "It"—took over. I turned around to go back in there and tell this guy that he should give me at least some of the money back so that I could go score some drugs. Note what I'm saying here: I wasn't going to ask the guy to give me back my money because it was wrong for him to take it and I needed it for my family. I was going to tell him that I needed a few dollars to go get a hit. But when I turned around to go back in, that man shot that gun right at me. He missed, thank God.

When I got back to the car and looked at the driver and the guy in the backseat, I said to myself, "You set me up." But I knew, too, that I deserved what I got, and God was right there protecting me. Ironically, every one of those guys who set me up that day is dead. Even the guy who robbed me—he went to prison, came out, and got killed. They didn't hurt me at all because even at my lowest, I was in God's grace, even when I didn't deserve to be.

. . .

The person who suffered the most through all of this was my mother. She had a chance to stick her chest out when her boys made it big, but when I got busted once or twice on account of my habit and it made the newspapers, the shame rained down. I felt horrible for her. She saw all of that. It was all the worse because she was saved and sanctified and filled with the Holy Ghost and she never drank, smoked, or cursed; she'd never remarried after my father left or even had another boyfriend.

More, she was in that church and people were jealous of her because of her sons' fame and because she was a strong-willed woman who was undeterred by setbacks. But we all knew better: there was no fortune, and the fame was fading fast, because everything got progressively shoddier with Total Experience. The worse the relationship, the more I depended on the drugs to get me through. The same thing that my mother's mother predicted would happen to her if she sang secular music is exactly the curse that befell her sons. We each struggled with some form of addiction. Mama was absolutely, categorically undone.

She traveled to California once, right after we decided we had to break with Total Experience. My mother wanted to sit and talk to me and my brothers about the lawsuit we'd filed against the label to recoup our money and what we were prepared to do to get ourselves together after we left the organization. But we were so high and so busy trying to do more drugs when we met up with her at the studio that every time she would run up the stairs to talk to us, we would run down the back way. Finally, she cornered Lonnie and told him straight and plain: "You built your empire with my sons' money and I'm going to live to see it crumble."

"Ms. Wilson," Lonnie said, "I never stole a red nickel from your sons."

My mother said, just as quick: "I know you didn't steal any red nickels because nickels ain't red. But as God is my witness, I'm going to see you crumble." She then turned to me and said, "Now take me back to the hotel."

I even tried to do a solo album, thinking that if I did it on my own, I could make the money we needed to get the group back together, with enough cash to do right by all of us. But whatever vocal I laid down, no matter what I recorded or how it sounded, Total Experience, which still had me under contract, would release it. There were even a bunch of songs I recorded on equipment I brought over to a hotel that Total Experience released as GAP Band songs; on some of them, you could hear the maid's vacuum running in the background. Total Experience released those songs on *The GAP Band VI*, *The GAP Band VII*, and *The GAP Band 8*, along with songs my brothers and I had recorded together and left in the vault because either we didn't care for them or they simply didn't make the cut on our previous albums. And there was nothing we could do to stop it because Total Experience paid for the hotel, studio time, and equipment. The quality of the music and songs made it seem like we were so high, we didn't know how to record anymore. The word in the industry was that we were just fucked up. It was nasty.

Ronnie and I ended up partnering to press a lawsuit against Lonnie. We had an agent at the Norby Walters Agency, then one of the top management firms, with three hundred acts, and he convinced Norby to loan Ronnie and me $100,000 to hire a litigator to get us out of that contract and recoup all the money we thought Lonnie owed us. The sticky part was that our little brother, Robert, refused to leave Total Experience Records. Robert believed that there was money still to be made with them and he was standing firm in that. The judge said something like, "You're telling me you gave this guy nine albums and that you haven't gotten anything from that, and that the other guy took it. But still, your brother is working with him." He seemed perplexed. "Is he being threatened? If he's broke, why is he over there with the man you're suing, instead of over here with his brothers?"

To make it worse, our one lawyer was up against a Goliath team of fifteen. Finally, Ronnie said, "We don't want anything. We just want out. We're never going to get paid anyway. Just give us our name." That was the worst decision he could have made. We didn't get any money but we got out of the contract. We settled that case in 1994, with each of us agreeing to walk away. I was free to sign with a new label.

It didn't take long before what little money I had dried up. I surrendered my home and car soon after. I couldn't keep up with the payments because I couldn't find work; nobody wanted to be bothered with us. Capitol Records approached us with a deal, but even with the settlement and Total Experience behind us, we couldn't close a deal with the company's wary executives.

We were relegated to booking shows on our own. By then, Ronnie had left the group to pursue a career in theater. Robert took over booking duties, but he was getting us incredibly low fees at small venues unworthy of our stature. We'd get offered three thousand dollars to play a small club—enough to buy a little meat and milk. Not much else. More than being beneath our worth, it didn't make financial sense. By the time we divvied up everything between us and our band and stagehands, we practically owed the venues money. It was as if I were back at A Blue Monday again, working to pay off a tab. Except this time, I wasn't a kid. I was a grown man with responsibilities and needs and enough hit records to know that things should have been different—to know that everything was horribly, tragically off. We were essentially starved out of making a living and went from famous but broke to literally homeless practically overnight. My singing career was over.

That was when I made the turn from hard-core drug user to stone-cold addict. The drugs and alcohol dulled the pain—made me forget in those hazy moments that the thing that gave me my identity, my ability to perform for others, was gone. Soon enough, I was out on the streets—a junkie, depending on a network of drug dealers, pimps, prostitutes, and homeless people to shelter me and to get me my fixes.

I avoided homeless shelters because people knew me and I still had hit records on the radio. Hollywood Boulevard was my haunt. I had a network of places that I called home; some were back alleys in the nooks of Los Angeles's most infamous street. Other times, I would head to a U-Haul parking lot, where I'd find makeshift shelter under the cabs of empty trucks. A lot of homeless people did the same; it was the perfect temporary accommodation if you wanted to stay out of sight and reasonably protected from the elements. My spot was beneath a truck in the back of the lot. The trucks up front would get rented first thing in the morning, forcing whoever was sleeping beneath them to gather their things and head out so that the trucks could move. My spot in the back gave me great cover; it allowed me to escape being exposed as homeless, plus I didn't have to rush out early in the morning.

I also found both company and safety in a shelter made up of shopping carts and plastic tarps that a homeless couple let me share with them. There, I slept on a cardboard box with a brick for a pillow.

I didn't eat out of garbage cans, but if that homeless couple

had a sandwich, they shared it with me and I would eat it because they were sanitary. I trusted that what they were putting
in their mouths was safe enough and clean enough for mine.

They were among only a handful of people who knew I had
nowhere to go. I never told anyone about my situation. Not even
the drug dealers and prostitutes and pimps who took care of me
knew I was down-and-out. Remember: Lonnie was still releasing GAP Band albums, so besides our string of hits, there was
also new GAP Band material on the radio, and really, no one
was the wiser. Dealers gave me drugs because they thought I
was still on top. They figured I was trolling for cocaine. If someone recognized me, I'd tell him I had just got out of the studio
and was on my way to the office and I just needed a little pick-
me-up to make it through the day. They'd say, "Come over to
my place and take a shower. I got some shit that'll wake you up
and you can go back to work."

I got a lot of favor because of who people thought I was. And
if anyone said anything out-of-order to me, then there were a
couple of guys who would look after me on that front, too. They
were deep in the life and hung in dangerous places—sometimes
dirty motel rooms, sometimes seedy, ramshackle houses on the
fringes of downtrodden neighborhoods overrun with the stench
of poverty, prostitution, and drug abuse. I didn't belong there.
I knew this. The dealers and their henchmen knew it, too. But
when I came knocking on their doors, they never, ever turned
me away. These were guys with two strikes against them and
not a care in the world about going to prison for twenty years to
life, but still, when I came into the room, they would launch into
these ridiculous sermons full of pleas and warnings—"Charlie!

If the police catch you here, you're going down!" Still, even as they recognized the dangers and risks I was taking to get high, my stardom was mesmerizing to them. They wanted to be around me as much as I wanted to be around them. We got high off each other.

It was easy enough for me to score. Even though I was strung out, people were willing to suspend disbelief and think I was a rich junkie. The pimps and drug dealers would leave me in the house with their money, their drugs, and their women, and when they got back, they would weigh up everything just to make sure I didn't stuff anything into my own pockets—or nose. I guess they were testing me. And once they saw everything was accounted for and they packaged what they needed, they would bag up what was left and say, "Here, Charlie, that's for you." I never did buy anything because I didn't have any money, but what I did have working for me was that trust—the kind of "favor" that would be returned with a "favor" I could put in my nose or smoke or drink. They made it so I could stay high. Even the crackheads were generous. They would say, "Charlie Wilson from The GAP Band!" and then make a place for me to sit, even if I didn't smoke a lot. I would stay there until it got dark, then, worried about wearing out my welcome, I'd say good-bye.

When I think about it now, about the benevolence of the people who, even at my darkest moments, treated me like I was still special, I remember how blessed I am. Though I didn't know it at the time, God covered me with his mercy, even when I didn't deserve it. Especially so. He had his angels camped all around me. Without them, surely, I would have died, as did this one man with whom I was smoking one time before he suddenly fell over dead. This guy hit the floor and nobody even looked up. Nobody called 911. I said, "Somebody go check on him!" But I couldn't get anyone to pay attention. Their attitude was, "Man, he always faints." Not this time.

And then there was the time I reconnected with this guy who lived in a huge mansion up in Beverly Hills, adjacent to the houses of celebrities I used to visit when I was on the road with The GAP Band, singing songs from the albums *The GAP Band II* and *The GAP Band III*, which were hot at the time; I would pull up, and like Scarface, he'd have a big mountain of drugs sitting out on the table. He'd take a Ziploc bag and drop a handful of a little something in it and roll it up and hand it to me. He was generous that way. One time I called him and whoever answered the phone said, "Come on over," so I went over to his place, anticipating a nice score. When I got there, the door was open and he was on the floor dead, with a bullet in his head. I turned around and ran the hell out of that house, trying not to touch any doorknobs because I have no doubt that had I shown up before he was killed or after the police were summoned, I would have been in a world of trouble. I watched from afar as they roped off that place and took the body away. It scared me to see that. But whereas something that traumatic could convince most people to quit full stop, my addiction wasn't having it. "It" wanted more, and the more drugs I did, the more reckless I became.

Nobody knew how far I'd sunk. But there I was, lower than I'd ever been, and mad about it. I was bitter and embarrassed about what I didn't have; I couldn't reconcile how it was that I could work so hard and end up with little more than a bad jones and a brick pillow.

Things got way worse before they got better. There was the one time I got busted in a drug kingpin's house just moments after he'd been told I was stealing his stash. People were stealing his drugs and blaming it on me, and I have no doubt that he was going to come at me for what he'd been led to believe I was doing. This guy was big-time; he had iron doors at the entrance of his home, bars on every window, and people working for him in every corner of the house, including women, because he was also a pimp. On this one particular day, I was upstairs sitting by the sliding door and he was lying on the bed, swarmed by prostitutes, and he just kept looking at me and shaking his head and saying over and over again, "Dog, why?" I didn't know what he was talking about and frankly didn't care. I was too busy smoking my pipe.

And then all of a sudden, there was a rush of feet and slamming doors and rumbles and noise, and before I knew it, there was a man standing over me with a gun. "Don't move, pop," he said.

I sat there looking; slowly, I blew out the flame in my pipe and stuffed it under the area rug where I was sitting. I thought he might be a rival drug dealer, there to take everyone out for whatever transgression may have occurred between crews, and I wanted to be ready to either fight or run, to do whatever I needed to do to keep out of harm's way. The kingpin knew immediately what was up: it was the police. "Aw, man," the kingpin said. "I don't have nothing in here. I got some little stuff, but not no big stuff worth all this here drama."

Once I figured out what was going on, I pulled my pipe back from up under that rug, lit it, and dropped another rock into it.

"Goddamn, man, you see me standing here?" the cop asked incredulously.

I was as honest as I could be for a crackhead: I said, "Man, if I'm going to jail, I want to get high before I go."

He turned around and looked at me with that hard glare. "Man, if you don't put that shit down . . . !" he demanded.

While he watched me put my pipe down, the kingpin was rolling around on the bed, trying to discreetly toss under the mattress a gun he had in his pocket. In the middle of all that commotion, all the prostitutes who were in the house got herded into the room by female cops who quickly set about frisking them.

"Well, look what we have here!" one of the officers said as she confiscated bags of drugs from the women.

The kingpin had an epiphany that would save me from future trouble with him: in that moment, he knew that it was his girls, not me, who'd been stealing from him. He was quick to apologize for mistrusting me, too. "Dog, I'm so sorry," he said. "I thought you were stealing."

"Man, I don't steal," I said insistently. And that was the truth. People used to lie and say, "Charlie got it," or "Charlie took it," because they figured no one would get mad at Charlie Wilson from The GAP Band.

I didn't go to jail behind that incident; they turned me loose because they were looking for something much bigger—kilos—and they already knew who they wanted to pin that on. I did, however, convince the cops to let me go back inside, under the guise that I needed to find my shoes. Here's how stupid I was: I was in there about thirty minutes, looking for rocks. I found some big ones, too. And I didn't care if I got busted. I just wanted them in my possession. That's what drugs do—they'll make you do some of the craziest things.

No matter how dark the times, I never forgot the power of prayer. In my makeshift shelters, in those crack dens, I used to pray to God, "Don't let the devil kill me out here like this, God. I don't want to die out here on these streets. Please don't let somebody kill me out here, and please don't let my family find me out here dead." Three years on the streets and that's the only prayer I ever prayed. When I reflect on that, I *know* God was surrounding me with people He sent specifically so that I would not get harmed. He was answering my prayers.

. . .

Rick James tried to save me. He was my brother—not by blood, but certainly in heart and spirit. He knew that I was in over my head, that if I didn't get right, those drugs would get ahold of me and take me out of here. "You need to be more Beverly Hills with the way you do that," he said to me once after we'd found ourselves in the same room doing the same drugs. He advised me to use them recreationally—to not go so fast. He knew, after all, from our earliest interactions that I was the quiet one, the guy who was more of a social misfit than the braggart who could stand out in an entourage fifteen people deep. On more than one occasion, he tried to slow me down, and more than once, he handed me the phone while saying, "Somebody wants to talk to you." I would pick it up and hear a voice on the other end of the line tell me, "Go home." I'd know immediately who that voice belonged to; it was so distinctive and pure and I've loved him a lifetime. It was Stevie Wonder. I'd look at Rick and say, "Aw man, you called Stevie on me? Like he's my daddy?" Stevie would just say it again: "Go home." Though Stevie and Rick and I had grown quite close, neither of them knew that I didn't have a home to go to. Or just how far gone I was. That's how closely I held my addiction and shame.

I also was quite reckless. One time I stayed up for ten days, and another time I stayed up for sixteen days, without food or water, just smoking drugs. In such a state, you don't notice if you're hungry or sleepy; you just don't care about anything, not even what you're smoking. The most minute things satisfied when it came to drugs. I could sit for three days in one person's house where some dope dealer would chop up drugs. When he was done, he'd sweep them up and say, "Here, Charlie, what's left is all you." Or he would put marijuana in a baggy and once it was almost full, he'd take whatever scraps he had left over and give them to me. Then I would go to somebody else's house to smoke for a couple days. That's how it was until it escalated from five days to ten days. I was so dehydrated, so high on a cocktail of booze and crack and marijuana and whatever else I could get my hands on, it would be hard for even a die-hard fiend to comprehend. I would lie down and eight or nine hours would pass with me wide awake, either doing drugs or thinking about doing them again. I was literally spiraling out of control, smoking all day, all night, sometimes alone, sometimes with Grammy Award–winning celebrities. Even they would say, "Charlie, you gotta eat," to which I'd respond, "I'm not hungry, I'm not sleepy—shut up and leave me alone." They would laugh and smoke and pursue their own high, leaving me to wallow in my own dysfunction. I'd rarely notice when they'd up and leave, but I'd be right there in the same place when they returned, sometimes three or four days later. I would have on the same clothes, while they'd freshened up. "Boy, you still here?" they would ask. When I was finally ready to leave, they would offer to take me home. "Just drop me off here, at this corner. I live right up in there," I'd say, the lies coming so easily.

I spiraled for sixteen days, until I collapsed and hit the pavement. People were rushing out of the house where I fell, yelling, "Oh my God, Charlie Wilson!" Of all the things I'd done that should have embarrassed me the most, falling over like a common junkie did me in emotionally. I couldn't admit to myself, let alone a street full of people, that Charlie Wilson, the singer whose music they'd come to love, was laid out in the street because he'd been on a drug binge. So I hollered out that some guy in a red plaid shirt hit me. The woman I was with started to say, "Nobody hit you—"

"Shut up!" I yelled.

She couldn't get the truth out because I wouldn't let her talk. They were combing the area for some guy who didn't even exist. Had anyone walked back there with a red plaid shirt, my friends would have beaten him to death. All I did was stand there, holding my head and nursing my swollen lip and my shame.

The hell I put my body through, the pain I caused my family, the embarrassment I brought to myself—I'm ashamed of all of it.

Chapter 7

She Saved Me

Addiction leaves a calling card with grotesque, telltale details: there is the shaking, as if the body can't contain its own poisons; the gray, pockmarked skin; the lifeless, hollowed eyes; the gaunt, dangerously thin body consisting of not much more than skin and bones, doing that awkward dance, in desperate search of that bell ringer. I was there. Shirley, my cousin, had been there, too, dancing in lockstep with me in the shadows of the fifteen-block radius around the corner of Hollywood Boulevard and Argyle Avenue, where we would smoke and drink and stay high together.

But when I ran into Shirley in Hollywood one fateful day, she wasn't doing that death dance anymore. Her skin, once dark and full of irritated blotches, was clear. Glowing. Dressed nicely, her hair smooth, Shirley looked good. She was clean. I was happy to see her and she was happy to see me, too, but her eyes and those tears she cried as she folded me into her embrace betrayed the alarm coursing through her heart and her bones and her sinews. She was not crying tears of joy at seeing her cousin after three long years. Her tears were laced with fear. Panic. She knew that I wouldn't have long on this earth if I didn't get help—fast.

"Give me a hit," I croaked into her ear, sure I could score a little something from her out there on the street.

"I'm clean, Charlie. Have been for three years," she said, her voice cracking.

"Three years?" I yelled, incredulous. The thought of three years having gone by since she and I had gotten high together blew my mind. I didn't know that I'd been in hell that long. For addicts, time doesn't exist.

While I contemplated that very thought, Shirley started to full-on cry, her face contorted, tears leaving streaks down her cheeks and chin. "I look that bad?" I asked, lucid enough to know that her tears were for me.

"You're going to die," she said, shaking her head. "I just don't want you to die. Look here, I work at this rehabilitation center. It's north of Los Angeles. You have to come in. You have to come with me, Charles."

"Rehabilitation center? North of LA? That's a long way away from here," I said almost reflexively as I considered the thought of being off the streets and thus cut off from drugs and the people from whom I could score them.

Shirley was undeterred. "Come with me, Charles. You're dying and you don't even know it."

I had already been to jail a number of times over what were considered minor offenses, all drug related, and each time, I was ordered to rehab by judges who, recognizing who I was and my vocation, gave me chance after chance to get clean and stay sober. But I squandered those gifts. I would hope with every fiber of my being that when I got released, I could get myself and my life together. But addiction made me feel like being sober wasn't a gift at all—that the true reward was in that smoke, in the high. That temptation was so strong that I could have been in a burning house and if there was some cocaine in the room where the fire started and it was almost burned to a crisp, I was going to run in there and get the last bit of it if I could. No matter how badly I wanted to turn myself around, I could not stay off the drugs and alcohol. I heard all those judges and accepted their second and third chances, and I would follow their orders and go to rehab for a few short days and then go hiding somewhere until a car full of people I knew would come through. I'd join them, and inevitably someone would have drugs and I would be off and running until I'd get caught standing on the street once again by police officers who would swing by and catch me up in the net. "Everybody get your hands in the air!" would penetrate the silence. And there I stood, waiting to give my name, knowing that the moment I said, "Charles Wilson," I'd be headed back to jail because I had bench warrants stacking up on me, the consequence of leaving court-ordered rehab. It was one continuous, exhausting loop.

Yet, somehow, seeing myself through my cousin's lens was an eye-opener for me.

I was in denial—really a mess. I was sick and tired of being sick and tired. I didn't want any more of the running and the hiding, the slinking through the shadows. Looking into Shirley's eyes, I saw options. I saw death and I saw life.

I chose life.

Shirley went to work that day and talked to the program director, a woman named Mahin, and asked if there was any way I could come in there and get clean. The waiting list at the rehab center was long, but they managed to get me into a twenty-eight-day program—the only one that was available, as the ninety-day and six-month programs were full. The next day, Shirley sent a friend of hers to fetch me from whatever hole I was in and bring me to the program. I got in the car with her because I had made a promise to myself that I would go, but I had Shirley's friend drive me around that rehab center for close to a half hour while I smoked all the crack I could get into my system. Finally, the woman said she wasn't going to drive around any longer; she stopped in front of that rehab and I walked in, completely unaware that I was walking into a new life.

Words cannot express how scared I was when I first walked through those doors. I was high, I had drugs and paraphernalia in my bags, and I hadn't detoxed, a key requirement to entering the program. I was able to circumvent the scrutiny typically given new patients because I was a celebrity and my cousin worked at the facility, but being unaccountable to the rules in place to help patients realize a successful journey toward sobriety made my work that much harder. This was not going to be some cakewalk. The prospect of being caught with drugs and, even more, failing and heading back to the streets the same way I'd left them had me shook.

But rather than focus on what was important, I trained my sights on superficiality. The first thing I did when I settled into my room was dye my hair blond. I saw a guy there who had done the same; it looked good on him. I asked him if he could do mine, too. He happily obliged. Picture me, standing at five feet eleven inches, weighing about 115 pounds—about as much as I weighed in the seventh grade—with ugly, pockmarked, dry skin and bright blond hair. I looked like a matchstick. I was ugly as hell. When you're homeless, there aren't many opportunities to preen in the mirror. I hadn't seen myself in a mirror for at least a year, and the last time I had gazed at my own reflection, I was in some guy's house and using the bathroom. I looked like a deflated balloon. All I wanted to do was go and hide, I looked so bad. But that blond hair at rehab made me feel like something. Like somebody. I was hiding behind that hair. It made me stand out—made me look like a star. And that allowed me to hide behind my celebrity in a way that I wouldn't have been able to do if no one knew I was Charlie Wilson from The GAP Band. Subconsciously, this was important. Because, in all honesty, I was in a rehab, but I wasn't ready to rehab. I was consumed with fear of the unknown and still jonesing for my safe place: life on the streets, where the three addictions I craved most—crack, alcohol, and recognition for being a star—were satisfied. Something as simple as having a shock of weird-colored hair allowed me to keep pretending that I was Charlie Wilson, the star of The GAP Band, rather than a common junkie.

With my new look I started my classes. On day one of the twenty-eight days, I fell asleep. Same thing on the second day, though that time, I was more tired than I was bored, no doubt because my body was detoxing. On the third day, just before class, I was about to take some of the drugs I had snuck into the facility when I heard footsteps coming down the hallway. I put the stuff up just before I heard the knock on the door.

It was a counselor, the guy who lived across the hall from me. "Hey, man, I heard you were here—just wanted to introduce myself and tell you welcome," he said. We exchanged pleasantries and then he went on his way. I waited about ten minutes, then I got my stuff out and tried to smoke it again, only to hear more footsteps coming down the hallway. I hid the drugs a second time. The rap on the door belonged to Mahin, the program coordinator.

"I'm glad to have you," she said before calling me out: "I heard you were falling asleep in class."

"Wow, she's cute," I thought as I pulled myself out of a daze long enough to hear her say she was going to keep an eye on me and that I should get as much as I could out of the classes.

"I—I will," I stammered as I watched her walk out the door.

Still, the next day, I feel asleep again. As my body detoxed, it simply couldn't handle being alert; I hadn't had any real food or rest for God knows how long, and now my body was rebelling.

I went the first ten days without participating in the program. I didn't get it. I didn't want to. And once people found out who I was, I went out of my way to be the celebrity they expected. I may not have had a stage or a microphone, but I certainly put on shows. I was taking pictures and signing autographs all the time, yet when it came time for classes, I wouldn't say anything. I refused to share. I wasn't about to say, "I'm Charlie Wilson, and I'm an alcoholic and a crackhead and a cocaine addict." It took me a long time to come to grips with what I'd become. Besides, I wasn't one to tell my life story to anybody. I was not ready to let people know that Charlie Wilson, that guy they'd heard on the radio and whose picture and autograph they wanted, was homeless and so severely dysfunctional that he had no place to go and was sleeping in precarious places, hanging with pimps and prostitutes and drug addicts, and smoking the rocks in the dirt and the droppings drug dealers left behind as they packed up their stashes. I simply couldn't bear to have people put me on a pedestal, only for me to sit there and say, "No, that pedestal does not exist."

Instead, I focused on how I was going to get that hit I was craving. This was not going to be easy; the staff was charged with testing us patients and searching our rooms to make sure we weren't violating our promise to stay clean while undergoing treatment, so there was a huge chance that I could get tossed out of the program if caught. My need for drugs was much more powerful, however, than the fear of being found out—at least at that particular time.

The first moment I thought it was safe to do so, I pulled out my stash to smoke. But I couldn't find my pipe. Not anywhere. It wasn't anything special—nowhere near the beautiful pipes I'd seen some of my Beverly Hills friends smoking from. Mine was a street shooter—all chipped up at the ends with dirty screens. But it was mine and I wanted—needed—to have it.

As I searched furiously for that glass, something really shiny captured my eye. It looked like a kaleidoscope swallowing the light of the sun. There were a million reflected points of light in tiny little fragments; it almost looked as if someone had poured salt or sand onto the floor. I could see my crack rock still, but the rest of what had been my pipe was gone.

It was a sign: God broke my crack pipe into a million pieces— His way of saying, "You won't smoke it ever again." It was a message just for me—an answer to my prayers to God to help me finally get clean and sober. In that very moment, right there among the shards of that glass pipe, I realized God was speaking directly to me, telling me that He was going to honor my prayer and take away my addiction. In those moments, I chose to listen to Him. I was going to put down the drugs and alcohol and follow Him.

I ran out of the room and into this guy I'd seen around; I invited him back to my place, promising him he could have my stash. "I don't want it, but I don't have anything for you to smoke it with," I said. So he went and got a Coca-Cola can, which he rigged in some kind of way so that he could smoke the rock, right there in my room. The smell made my stomach turn. It smelled foul. Disgusting. I wanted to get away from it, to get that putrid smell out of my nose. Plus, I knew it was wrong for this guy to be smoking, especially in my room; if anyone smelled even a hint of that crack, we would both be tossed out on our behinds.

"You know what? I think you ought to take it with you," I said. "This is not right."

I managed the willpower to walk away from temptation that time, but I knew I couldn't fight it by myself—the battle wasn't mine to win alone.

Addiction is forever. I will always have this disease. The moment I had that realization, I understood that one hit, one drink, is too many, and a thousand is never enough. I didn't want to believe this in the beginning; I thought I could stop anytime I wanted to. But the reality is, addiction had a strong hold on me, and every time I had left rehab, those demons would take over and I wouldn't be able to fight them. But I had to do the work to get clean and change the habits that kept me addicted.

Later that day, I went to class and the counselor said, "Mr. Wilson, you haven't said much in the last couple weeks. Why don't you share?" Finally, I broke down, because everything that everyone else had been saying all along sounded exactly like what I was feeling. Everybody, after all, has the same story: "I smoke too much"; "I hate myself"; "I see myself in the mirror and I can't stand it." Then they start talking about all the people who are disappointed in them or the things somebody does to them and how they use all of that as an excuse to get high. Those were all the things I was doing. I'd think about my father and how he left when I was thirteen, and I'd think about all the people who'd betrayed me, and I would wallow in self-pity. I would think about all those contracts I'd signed and how the thing that once brought me so much joy—singing and writing music—now brought me only pain. In my mind, everyone else had their beautiful families, their beautiful homes, their beautiful lives. All I had was an excuse I used to make all the time: "I ended up with the short end of the stick." It was time to face the music: *I let all those bad things happen.* I realized, finally, that I was blaming other people for all of my failures, yet they were mine alone. And the only way I was going to heal was to let it all go. To give myself over to Him. That was an epiphany for me. It cracked wide open the shield I'd had up for so long. The key to my sobriety was being honest with myself—admitting I had a problem. I didn't want to say, "My name is Charlie Wilson and I'm an alcoholic addict." But the first time I said it, I felt as if one hundred pounds had been lifted from my shoulders. I broke down and started crying and released things I'd had pent up for years: the pressure I had trying to be as good as my sister and brother who came before me in school, and how happy it made me that my teachers believed in me and my talent enough to give me special privileges; how devastated I was when my old man left our family; how I'd been a fool in business, signing contracts I did not fully understand and signing away my music.

From that moment forward, I got stronger. When someone graduated from the program, I would ask for details on how long they'd been there and what they looked like when they got there. Always, it would be something like, "She wasn't but ninety pounds when she got here. Now she weighs one hundred and forty. She looks good, doesn't she? Her hair isn't nasty anymore." Then I would ask for more details about their trajectory. Every time someone graduated, I could see myself on the other side. The more I witnessed it, the more I wanted to be clean.

About fourteen days in, I heard footsteps coming down the hallway toward my door again—this time, light ones. It was Mahin, the program director.

"I want to talk to you," she said. "Come to my office after you get out of your next set of classes."

"Yes, ma'am," I said nervously, wondering what I'd done wrong to get called into her office.

A few hours later, I was standing in front of Mahin's office, tapping lightly on the door. She beckoned me in; her dog, Tasha, growled at me.

"Aw, don't be like that," I said to the dog. She was on a chain, so I moved a little closer to her and held out my hand so she could smell me. "Come here."

And just like that, the dog moved a little closer and let me rub her.

"Wow," Mahin said, amazed. "My dog never goes to anybody. She just tries to bite their faces off."

"Well, I like dogs," I said. And this was the truth. I'm an Oklahoma boy; my love of animals comes naturally. We didn't grow up on a farm, but we had plenty of friends whose families had horses and cows and chickens. Animals were a part of our everyday lives. In fact, I, too, had a dog named Tasha, same as Mahin's.

"Looks like Tasha likes you a lot," Mahin said.

"Hey, before we talk, you mind if I take her outside for a walk? She can use the bathroom while we're out there."

"Go right ahead," she said.

We stayed out for a few minutes, walking in the sun, Tasha bouncing around my feet as I rubbed her fur. She was happy. And for that moment, I felt . . . free.

I walked Tasha back into Mahin's office and reattached her to her chain, then sat and waited to hear what Mahin had to say to me.

"I've been getting reports on you and your classes," she said. "Let me ask you a question: Fourteen days have already gone by and you only have two weeks left. Where are you going when you get out?"

This isn't such a hard question for people whose lives haven't been completely dismantled by their addiction: perhaps they have families to go back to, or a significant other, or a friend who loves them and still believes in the good in them. But for those drug addicts whose lives have been obliterated due to their sickness, going home isn't an option. There is no one to love. Nowhere to call home. There are only the streets and the very people who are invested in your spiral back down to rock bottom. I had no money, no home, no transportation. The woman I had been seeing when I went into rehab was a drug dealer, and most of my family members were also involved with drugs. Being anywhere around any of them would have been a recipe for disaster. The only way I could continue my sobriety was to stay far away from the people with whom I used to get high. This is a key condition of sobriety for recovering addicts: those who end up cavorting with the same people and in the same environments that enabled their addiction have an almost impossible time staying clean—not just because their will is weak, but also because all too often, the people who enabled your addiction won't like the new, sober you and will try to find ways to make you relapse. Understanding this in that moment, I became keenly aware that all the progress I'd made in just two weeks under the care of this particular rehab center could disappear within moments of my walking out that front door. The thought of this hit me like a ton of bricks. Within seconds of being asked the question, I was in tears.

It was embarrassing to cry in front of this woman. But Mahin was unmoved. A no-nonsense person, she hadn't called me into her office for chitchat; she wanted to know what was my endgame. She cared about this not just because it was her job to do so—her responsibility was to help and guide patients through successful discharges from the facility—but because she is a kind woman who, in addition to being sincere about the recovery of her charges, had a soft spot for me because I was Shirley's cousin. Having helped Shirley get clean and sober and find a job at the rehab facility, she wanted to do the same for me.

"Where are you going to go when you get out?" Mahin repeated.

"I don't have anywhere to go, Mahin," I said when I could finally get the words out. "I don't know where I'm going to go after I finish here."

Mahin sat, quiet, then finally made an offer: "Well, your cousin Shirley says I should help you, and if I could help you, it would be good, because you're a good person and sincere about your recovery. She believes in you."

"Man, if I could just get this one thing right, I promise I will try to do this the right way," I whispered. "I'll get out of this life."

"Okay, we'll see," she said. "We'll talk again soon."

I went back to my room and fell down on my knees. My prayer to God was straightforward, insistent, and clear: "God," I prayed hard, "take this disease away from me. Make me sober and whole and give me the strength and courage to stay that way. Do this for me, Lord, and I promise that I will always share my story with anyone who can hear the words coming out of my mouth. Get me back to the stage and I will keep your name on my tongue and tell everyone in my audiences going forward about your goodness and mercy and what you did for me."

I prayed that prayer for two days and trusted that God would hear me.

A few more days passed by before Mahin summoned me

back to her office again. "I want to help you," she said. "First, we have to find you a place to live."

I furrowed my brow, unsure of whether I'd heard her correctly. But once I digested the words, I burst into a wide grin. When she said she would find me a place to live, the aura around her face started to glow. She looked like an angel.

"Oh my gosh, you'll find me a place to live?" I asked, excited.

"Yes. I'll get you a pass and we'll go out. I'm happy to help."

Before long, we did just that. Mahin piled me into her car and we took off in search of my new start. But I'll tell you, the devil was on me, trying to convince me that nothing would be good enough unless it involved my being Charlie Wilson from The GAP Band again. I was intent on being a star, and in my mind, a star needed a fifteen-bedroom house in a swank neighborhood—one that I could truly call my own, without anyone else's name on the mortgage.

Mahin let me hold on to the thought but she knew instinctively that the last thing I needed was what I was looking for. Finally, we found our way into this one area that was a few steps lower than what I had in mind. I turned my nose up immediately. "This neighborhood is kinda eh," I sniffed. But then, finally, it hit me. I can't explain what it was; I can only describe it as a really sharp pain that I felt vibrate from the back of my eyes up through the top of my head. That was God.

"What's wrong?" Mahin asked.

"Nothing," I said, rubbing my eyes as we pulled up in front of a house that was for lease. It was four bedrooms, two stories, about three thousand square feet, with a three-car garage. Nice by most people's standards. As I made my way through the house, with Mahin by my side, I quickly realized it was just the speed at which I needed to run.

"Is this okay?" she asked.

"Man, this is perfect," I answered.

Mahin leased that house for me out of her own pocket, and the next day, she took me furniture shopping and, with her own money, filled that house with everything I needed to be comfortable—a couch, a bed, chairs, and a table. She didn't have to do this; I was, after all, a complete stranger who also was an addict. But Mahin wasn't just doing her job for a paycheck; she was intent on helping people like me and Shirley because she could see straight through to our hearts. I could not believe the generosity of this woman who barely knew me and wanted absolutely nothing in return, save that I would take my recovery seriously. But here was Mahin, this angel that God sent to help me get myself together. I knew from her actions and expectations that He was sending me a clear and powerful message: Mahin was providing the opportunity for me to get sober and back on my feet. And I shouldn't squander the blessing.

I was hoping she would get me a car, too, but she didn't ignore my hints so much as explain why that was a horrible idea. "Change doesn't happen right away," she said while we took a break from furniture shopping. "It takes time. Let me show you: give me your watch."

Unsure of what point she was going to make or why my watch was involved, I hesitated, but eventually I gave her my timepiece.

"Now put it on your other arm," she said, handing it back.

I did.

About an hour passed before she asked me the time. Without hesitation, I looked at the empty wrist on which I always wore my watch. Habit.

"See how you automatically looked for your watch on that arm? Your subconscious acted so fast that it made you look for your watch on the arm you knew it wouldn't be on. That same subconscious will take you to places it's used to going and around people it's used to being around because it is not yet fully trained to think differently. If I got you a car, you'd use it and your subconscious would lead you straight to the liquor store or somewhere else that's just too dangerous for a recovering drug addict. You will end up somewhere you don't want to be."

Although I'd been in rehab for only about three weeks, I was sober and lucid enough to know that I was walking on thin ice— that my sobriety was wholly dependent on sheer will and the counseling tools that were designed to help me beat my habit. Stay away from my old haunts. Definitely stay away from the people at those old haunts. Swap out friends and family members who drink for new people who care about me enough not to bring liquor and crack anywhere near me. Know my triggers and do what it takes *not* to push buttons that would convince me to self-medicate to dull the pain. As a program director at a rehab, Mahin, too, knew all the tricks and pitfalls, all the ways an addict could climb out of the gutter, only to find himself just one drink, one snort, one cigarette, one toke away from relapse. So I fell on my knees and thanked God that she was right there by my side, as skinny, addicted, and penniless as I was.

As if she hadn't already provided enough strength, courage, and support to get me back on the road to sobriety, Mahin helped me all the more when she agreed to accompany me to a gig my younger brother had booked for The GAP Band. By then, Shirley had spread the word to him and other family members that I was in rehab, and so he knew where to find me. I had only about four days left in rehab, but I still needed permission to go work. More important, I desperately needed a support system that would put up a force field between me and the temptation that was sure to come when I got back into show business, where liquor, drugs, and bad behavior are available in abundance. My sobriety was too new, too fresh. Too fragile. I was determined to do right, but I wasn't dumb enough to think I could make it all on my own. Scared of the prospect of being sucked back into the darkness, and fully aware that my little brother was still getting high, I asked Shirley and Mahin to come with me, which they thankfully agreed to do.

The stage was my safe zone, but backstage was a disaster waiting to happen. It's always full of clingers-on and men of unclear purpose whose sole desire is to hang around with celebrities and see what kind of insanity and havoc they can bring and get into while they're back there. Liquor and drugs flow in abundance. People try to score some for themselves or to make a quick buck by selling it to anybody who may have some money in their pockets. Basically, it's ground zero for addiction—just the place I didn't need to be with only twenty-four days of sobriety behind me. And sure as rain is wet, the sun is hot, and my skin is chocolate brown, there they were, a bunch of vultures waiting to swoop down on me and reel me back into that dark place I was trying so hard to escape. One guy walked right up to me and shook my hand, leaving a huge crack rock in my palm.

"Man, I don't do drugs anymore," I said, shaking my head and handing the rock back to him.

"I heard that," he said.

"Well, if you heard that, why are you trying to give me drugs?" I asked.

"Aw man, I just wanted to see if it was true or not," he said easily.

As invested as I was in staying clean, it was clear that these people couldn't have cared less about my desires or what was best for me. They were jackals, and I was the prey. Clearheaded for the first time in ages, I could understand. I was like a horse in a barn full of excrement, whipping his tail to shoo away all the flies drawn to the stink. It is rather impossible to do business when you have flies in your face. I made the right call bringing my support system. Mahin, a no-nonsense person who had the strength to stand up for my sobriety when I couldn't, minimized the flies. She and Shirley also isolated me from the people they knew were users and wanted me to get high with them or buy their drugs.

Taking it a step further, on the ride back to the rehab center that night, we decided that I wouldn't get onstage for some time to come. Another good thing that came from my first concert during my recovery was that Mahin had met Robert, and she declared upon seeing him that she would get him into rehab soon enough. Eventually, she did.

About a week or so after the concert, it was time for my graduation from the twenty-eight-day program. I looked good—

certainly better than I had upon entering the facility. I had put on a little weight, my skin was clearing up, some of my color was back, and I was rested.

I should have been proud—and I was—but I was scared, too. That night backstage confirmed for me that I wasn't ready to be by myself as I continued my recovery. I couldn't think of a better person to have with me than Mahin. After all, she was a walking rehab—just the kind of person who could keep me in check and help me avoid the backslide. What's more, I was falling in love with her. My God, she was so smart and kind and honest and straightforward with me, and, on top of that, she was just a beautiful woman with a beautiful spirit. I was very clear on this one true thing: I *wanted* Mahin. She came from a good family and had a good background. She had no fear of expressing her feelings and did so in an assertive manner, and encouraged me to do the same. "Not everyone is your friend," she said insistently, spreading her special brand of much-needed tough love through all aspects of my life. How would I be able to do anything without her?

So I set about getting her. I just kept on nagging and begging her, and talking to and nagging her some more. I was always terrible when it came to sweet-talking the ladies; the music, the lyrics, the celebrity always got me over and into their beds. But for Mahin, I was going to have to show her my heart. How else was I going to win over this beauty? I was an addict, gaunt and ugly after years of letting drugs and alcohol take their toll on my body. I had nothing to offer her—not a pot to piss in or a window to throw it out of, except for the one that she'd taken care to secure. Still, I had to try.

"Come live with me," I said one day while I was sitting in her office.

"Live with you?" she asked. "I don't even know you."

"Regardless of if you know me or not, I'm going to ask you to marry me one of these days soon," I said confidently. "We're meant to be together."

"But I don't know you," she repeated.

I poured it on thick. "Does anybody know anybody when they get married?" I asked. "Look, I can't be over there at that house by myself. I'm telling you, that place is like a devil's workshop. My mind is going to wander and I'm going to search for somebody with whom to get high. I need you. You make me want to do better. You make me want to be better. I don't want to do this without you." I pulled out all the charm I could muster. My life depended on it. I knew that without Mahin, I would die. I knew that if I went back out into the world all alone, without the benefit of her strength and guidance, in no time I would go back to using drugs and alcohol, which would lead me right back to the streets—right back to sleeping beneath that U-Haul truck in the very back of the lot. My grave. I was but one drink, one hit away from that reality. Mahin was helping me to be stronger than I could ever have been otherwise in those early moments of my sobriety. I needed her. And I wanted her to be with me until our dying days.

She didn't answer right away. In fact, I asked her several times more—more than either of us can remember. But Mahin said she was not ready to be my wife. Instead, she set about supporting me in every way possible, from shooing away friends and family who still used, to turning away people who had stolen from me, to constantly talking to me about staying strong. She even supported me in court one time when I had to answer for a summons I'd gotten while I was still on the streets. The judge, tired of ordering me to rehab, told my attorney that he was finished being lenient with me and wanted me to do some time in prison. There I was, sitting on a bench listening to my attorney, feeling as small and frightened as anyone could feel at the prospect of losing his freedom, when Mahin burst through the courtroom's heavy wooden doors, pushing past the guard, and taking off toward the judge.

"Ma'am, you can't go up there!" the guard said insistently, grabbing her by the arm.

"Let her approach," the judge said after seeing all the commotion. "It's okay."

Mahin wasted no time before pressing into his hands a business card and a letter she'd written on my behalf, detailing my progress and noting that I was receiving drug counseling and using my spare time to go to schools to talk to kids about my career and all the ways I'd fallen because of my addiction to alcohol and drugs. "Sending him to jail would not help him at all," Mahin said insistently.

By now, the prosecutor was on his feet, protesting Mahin's request. But the judge wasn't listening to him; instead, he was staring at Mahin's business card. "You know, one of my family members was in rehab at this facility," he said. "He's sober now. That place changed his life."

After a few more moments, the judge looked right at me and showed me the mercy for which Mahin had advocated. "Mr. Wilson," he said, "I'm going to grant you the chance to prove how serious you are about turning your life around. I want you to continue to get drug-tested to show that you are staying sober. Do that, and you can avoid prison time."

Again, Mahin had saved me.

After six months of giving all I had to continue with my sobriety and prove I was serious, I asked Mahin again if she would marry me. And, finally, she said yes. Yes!

"I'm going to have to quit my job. I can't marry a client and continue to work there. It's against company policy."

That made me bottom out. Quit her job? I didn't have any money—not even a bank account. "How am I going to take care of you? I have nothing."

"I know your heart. I can see you're a good person," she said. "You're going to have to do what I'm going to do, and that's put your trust in God and have faith that everything is going to be okay."

We have been together ever since.

. . .

Mahin and I were in love, but those first years were far from easy. While I was in rehab, the counselors had warned that I should stay far away from any kind of relationship for the first one or two years, so that I could work on myself, but there I was, in a committed relationship with a woman I hardly knew in one sense but instinctively knew was good for me. And I wanted to give her my best.

I stayed sober that whole first year while we lived together in the house she leased for us. Dealing with those demons that were trying to convince me to get high, I would sometimes pick fights and start arguments, not necessarily to get away from her, but with the hope that I could get out of the house and feed my jones. Love was one thing, but being there with Mahin was like being in rehab twenty-four hours a day, seven days a week. I hated that rehab mode; it was fine at the facility, but I didn't want it in my house. Family would call or stop by the house and she would tell them to go away; to me, it was family, but Mahin knew that those particular people were just there to use me.

"This isn't a bank," she would tell people who would ask for money.

"You can't go with them," she would say if someone asked me to go hang out with them.

"You're not going over to that club, sorry," she would say if she knew it was a place of ill repute.

Had I stayed in the rehab center for its ninety-day or one-hundred-and-twenty-six-day program, I would have understood what she was trying to do a lot quicker than I did, but I had only twenty-eight days there, and really, I'd only paid attention and put in my best effort fourteen days into that. I know it was rough on her, particularly as my family resented her keeping us apart. To make matters worse, her colleagues at the center were upset with her for leaving such a high-powered gig at which she excelled to take up, essentially, with a drug addict.

Just because I was starting to appreciate what she was doing for me doesn't mean it was smooth sailing. I remember one time picking a fight about nothing in particular and then walking out of our home with the keys, slamming the door behind me, while she was getting ready to get in the shower. By the time I got in the car and started the ignition, she was opening the passenger door, with nothing on but rollers in her hair. "If you're going, I'm going, too!"

"Get out of this car!" I yelled. But I couldn't keep the bass in my voice; I burst out in laughter. "You don't have any clothes on!"

"You don't, either," she retorted. "You're as naked as I am."

Sure enough, I was. We both looked at each other and started laughing hysterically. I looked in the rearview mirror, hoping none of the neighbors saw us two fools out there buck-naked, hollering and screaming and laughing like lunatics. They would have never understood what we had, what that moment meant to us. God was saying, "Listen. You got something here and you need to take care of it and roll with the punches. I gave you what you asked for." She was such a beautiful person and made my fight to stay sober and take care of myself all the more important to me. She made me want to be a better man. She didn't ask me for a single thing other than to be that for her. *A better man.*

In return, she cleared my life of the people, the places, and the things that threatened to suck me back into the darkness. She was nice to them at first, trying to make it work because I insisted that they were okay, but she knew that they weren't, and she helped me to understand that they didn't mean to do right by me. She knew it, even if I couldn't see it. There was a lot of grief behind that. These were people I cared about. But they didn't care about me. When I started performing again, they would try to suck me right back into the old habits that kept me high and them paid, but Mahin was there, making sure that they never touched me. When they couldn't get to my pockets by offering me drugs, they started picking my pockets instead. People would come backstage and steal checkbooks and money out

Me at seven years old.
P Music Group

My little brother and me on Christmas. *P Music Group*

In front of my childhood home before my last junior high football game. I enjoyed football until I discovered the marching band.

P Music Group

My high school graduation day.

P Music Group

Performing on *Soul Train* with my brothers in 1975.
Michael Ochs Archives/ Getty Images

Performing with The GAP Band in Chicago in 1983.
Raymond Boyd/ Michael Ochs Archives/ Getty Images

Enjoying the beach in Cannes, France, in 1983.
David Corio/Redferns

Singing with The GAP Band in Chicago in 1984. *Raymond Boyd/ Michael Ochs Archives/Getty Images*

My father and me.
P Music Group

The GAP Band being honored with the BMI Icon Award in 2005. *Rick Diamond/WireImage for BMI*

Me about a month before my cousin took me to rehab for my last time. *P Music Group*

With Mahin on our wedding day.
P Music Group

My mother and me.
P Music Group

Celebrating Zulu Ball in New Orleans
with Mahin. *P Music Group*

With Michael Paran and my brothers a
few years into when he started managing
The GAP Band. *Harry Langdon*

Snorkeling in St. Thomas right before
I thought I was going to be attacked
by a shark. *P Music Group*

Clowning around with
Lil Jon and R. Kelly. *Rick
Diamond/WireImage for BMI*

Performing with my
brothers in 2005. *Rick
Diamond/WireImage*

Having some fun with
Aaron and Damion Hall
from the group Guy.
*Rick Diamond/WireImage
for BMI*

Me with Snoop at Live 8 London in 2005. *Gareth Cattermole/Getty Images for AOL*

Performing with Snoop on *Idol Gives Back* in 2008. *Kevin Winter/Getty Images*

Snoop, Mahin, and me when Snoop asked his wife, Shante, to remarry him in a surprise ceremony at our ranch. *P Music Group*

Promoting my *Charlie, Last Name Wilson* album.

Getting on a plane with Mahin, headed to another base to perform for the US troops in Iraq in 2009. *P Music Group*

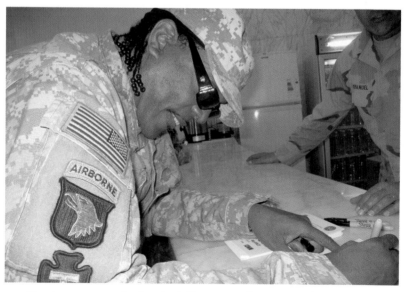

Signing autographs for the US troops after my performance in Iraq in 2009. *P Music Group*

of Mahin's purse and act as if they didn't know who did what. Before we knew what hit us, she had about fifteen thousand dollars stolen out of her account. Now, my wife is Persian, and she's a lover of people, very trusting. But you bite a Persian just one time, and you can forget it. They understand when a snake is a snake. Me, I'd have to be bitten ninety times to get it, which is why I would be comfortable, say, going to the bathroom and allowing my wife to leave her purse sitting around in the dressing room, trusting that my "friends" wouldn't do us like they did. Things like that could have broken us. But instead, they made us stronger. I understood that I had to protect this woman who really loved me. And she said no matter what, she was going to stand by my side and do the same for her husband.

When we both thought I was ready to get back to work, Mahin got rid of my lawyer and fired my agent and my road manager. She then set about trying to help my younger brother, Robert, too. Robert adored Mahin. He would call her Sister-in-law and she would respond in kind by treating him with the same respect she gave to me. She became our de facto manager for a while; she stepped in to help negotiate our contracts, pick up the money for our shows, and divide it evenly to the penny between Robert and me. Soon enough, we started booking more shows and Mahin tried her hardest to help us reclaim that GAP Band glory.

My brother Ronnie took notice, and one night when Robert and I had a show, he asked if he could join us onstage and play. After much discussion, we said yes. Our first show together captured some of the old electricity but also some of the drama. When it was time to divvy up the pay, Robert wanted to pay

Ronnie only five hundred dollars for his services. It was Mahin who insisted that the money be split into three equal portions; the first time they met was when she gave Ronnie his money.

Their bond was short-lived. The tenuous peace we'd achieved with the new GAP Band iteration became shaky immediately when Ronnie started coming on the road with us. In no time at all, he started to take control of The GAP Band's affairs and treat Mahin with little respect. I wasn't happy about that. He also hired a new manager for us—who Ronnie borrowed money from, then summarily fired, leaving me to pay back his loan out of my own pocket. To make matters worse, people were telling me that Ronnie was saying horrible things about me and my wife. Mahin would get upset, which, in turn, would get me upset. It was a rough time. But it was Mahin who counseled me to soldier on. We knew where we stood. That is all that mattered.

A year after Mahin and I got together, I was back on my feet with enough money to buy a place of my own. Though Mahin had predicted it, to me, it was a miracle. Just a year before, I didn't have a dime to my name. And now, here we were, driving through fancy neighborhoods, with me looking for a big house.

Mahin entertained my grandiose pronouncement that I was looking for a mansion while we were out searching, but eventually, she'd had enough. She asked me to pull over so that we could talk.

"Let me ask you a question," she said. "What do you want with a big house, and why do you want it?"

I stuttered and mumbled a few words, but really, I didn't have any kind of coherent answer to her very candid question.

"Let me tell you this," she said. "There won't be any big parties, there won't be lots of people coming and going. It's just me and you. The quicker you understand it's just me and you for the rest of our lives, the better. We won't need all of what you're searching for. You'll see that all you need is right here, with us."

I was blown away by that. I'd thought that things would be different once I got sober, but Mahin's assessment was correct: being sober for one year did not change the fact that I was a recovering addict. Things were not ever going to be the same, and that was a good thing. It took me some time to honor that, mainly because as a man, I wanted to be assertive and make important decisions for my wife and myself, such as where we would live together and how we would spend our money. The truth was that my track record as a decision maker was sketchy at best. My choices had led me down the dark path toward homelessness and addiction, and I did not want to go back to that life. Ever. I had no comeback for Mahin's declaration, except to acknowledge that I understood and that I was going to manage my wants and focus on our needs.

Not long after that, we were driving and came upon a particular place with flags snapping in the wind. She told me to turn, and I did, then she said to turn into a particular driveway, and I did that, too. I knew this was where I was supposed to be from the moment I saw the flags. It was clear as day. As He had with the shattered pipe, God was sending me a sign; He was right there by my side, as He's always been.

The owner of the house came out and introduced herself.

"How you doing?" I said back. "The Spirit told me to come in."

"Spirit?" she asked.

"Yes, the Spirit," I said, confirming it.

"Well, come on in and take a look around," she said, holding the door open so that Mahin and I could enter her place.

It was fully furnished and just beautiful—perfect for what Mahin and I needed. This was the place for us. The owner agreed. While we were there, another couple came in and inquired about the house, and the owner said with quickness, "I'm sorry, this house has already been purchased."

I said, "Wow, who bought it?"

She turned to me and said, simply, "Baby, where is your faith? You told me that the Spirit told you to come on in. The Spirit moved you for a reason: this is your house."

I was looking at her and saying to myself, "Who is this lady? And why is she being so kind to us?" While I was contemplating that, Mahin came back into the room and said, "You're right; this place is perfect for us."

We made quick work of trying to seal the deal, but a few days later, when we were trying to secure a mortgage, the company that was loaning us the money said we were fifteen thousand dollars short and couldn't buy the place. I was so upset over that. I turned around and walked out of that office and sat in the car, beating up on myself and asking why every time I tried to do something good, only bad things happened. Just when I had given up all hope and was feeling as low as I could feel, don't you know that lady walked out and asked me again: "Charles, where is your faith?"

"I don't know, ma'am," I said. "I'm just kind of fed up right now."

"Here, baby," she said, dangling the keys to her place in my face.

"Ma'am, I don't have time for light jokes right now. We don't have the money to buy your house. I'm fifteen thousand dollars short."

"Don't worry about it," she said insistently. "I'm going to give it to you. You have good things coming to you. That's what the Spirit is telling me."

I didn't know what to say. I had no words. Instead, I sat in that car, crying again like a little boy. There was no earthly reason for her to have given me or Mahin, two people she'd never met before, the money.

It was God's work.

I am a believer.

I never saw that angel again; she moved to Vegas and left that house to us and moved on with her life. It took us a while to pay her back, but we did.

That is how Mahin and I got started together. On faith. The Spirit led me to her and her to me.

Everyone around me recognized the changes in me, and most knew I couldn't have done it without Mahin. When Rick James got out of prison, I talked to him often about giving up drugs and hanging with me again, this time sans the spotlight and the cocaine and liquor and women and people who didn't mean to do right by him. I introduced him to Mahin, hoping that he would see us together and be inspired. He came by a GAP Band show one night and met me and Mahin in the dressing room. I was preening in the mirror, getting myself ready to go onstage, and I looked up over my shoulder and saw him there, just staring and crying.

"What's wrong?" I asked.

"You have an angel," he said, "and I don't."

I was quiet for a moment, contemplating what he was saying to me. I felt for my brother; I understood how tight that vise grip was on him.

I talked to him plenty of times after that. Rick would call me and ask me to sing to him and I would always offer up "You Can Always Count on Me," and he would cry and hang up. But he never did come and kick it with Mahin and me. All those years he tried to school me on how to do drugs, all the times he tried to save me from myself—in the end, he just couldn't save himself.

A couple of weeks before he died, he was telling me that his body was shutting down on him, that only 10 percent of his body parts were working. "I'm going to die a young Rick James," he said.

"Well, you should have died about thirty years ago, then," I joked.

"You can't talk to me that way," he said insistently, laughing.

Not long after that, he was gone. It hurt me so much when he died. Rick was more than just my friend; he was my brother. I loved him down to my core—not just Rick James the funk god, but Rick James the person. He was a beautiful man.

When we went to his funeral, I sat right behind Stevie as we said good-bye to our friend. I made a point of not going up to view him in the casket because I didn't want to remember him that way. Rick, walking with authority into a room, that spotlight on his every footstep—that's what I wanted to remember. But when I went to the studio to lay down some vocals a few days later, somebody showed me a picture of him in his casket, and seeing him like that bothered me for the longest time;

I even erased the song I was working on when I saw the picture, because every time I would try to sing it, I would think about my friend in that box, lifeless—a shell of the brightest star.

Rick needed an angel. I thank God that He sent me one. Mahin is my rock—the cool drink when I'm hot, my calm in the middle of chaos, the very beat of my heart. I could not imagine facing this life without her.

Chapter 8

The Voice

Even when I was high, even when I was on the streets, even when I had not one penny to my name, even when The GAP Band was no longer in rotation on the radio and we were fighting Lonnie, even when I wasn't sure I would live another day to see the sun kiss the dawn, the one thing I always had was music. Abusing drugs and alcohol destroyed my voice; out on the streets, I prayed that it would come back once I got sober. It did. This alone is a miracle, because years of alcohol and smoking could have easily destroyed my ability to make the noise. The vocal cords, after all, are not to be messed with. Neither are the lungs. Those layers of tissue, skin, ligaments, and vital organs I need to produce my unique sound easily could have been ruined by years of perpetual abuse, taken out by plaque from the smoke or dryness from the alcohol. The most serious consequence of all would have been losing the sensation that comes when the sound forms deep in the caverns of my belly and in my heart and rushes up through my throat and over my tongue and jaws and teeth and up to my audience, whether that be my fans or my Lord. When you are high or drunk, there is numbness—the absence of feeling, emotion, sensation—and making the noise sans these things is tantamount to singing way off key, akin to not being able to sing at all. Still, somehow, by the grace of God, after losing the physical and emotional connection to my instrument, I got it back.

I've long known that my voice is special—not just because people always told me so, but also because I worked hard at making it so. Of course, there are factors about the voice that one cannot control; you are literally born a singer or you are not. The shape of everything from the neck up determines whether you can sing well or whether you should stick to solo concerts in the shower: your nasal passages, how your teeth sit in your mouth, the shape of your cheeks, the way your tongue lies—all of these things and more work together to give those of us who sing the ability to make that pleasurable sound. But the soul, that thing that comes from down deep and bubbles to the surface, the thing that moves women to tears and inspires that guttural "yeah" from the men and gets everyone—the deacons, the grandmamas, the ornery neighbors, the music lovers, the fans all the way up in the nosebleed section, the quiet ones, and the sinners all—to feel it, takes serious work, and in the beginning, you have to literally cook up a stew of sounds to find your true voice.

When I first got into the business, I could blow, sure, but I wanted my fans to revere my voice like they did those of my musical heroes. Sam Cooke, James Brown, Marvin Gaye—I loved them all. But listening to Stevie Wonder's *Music in My Mind* album with headphones when I was a teenager changed my life—made me truly understand that God is in the vocal cords and distinctive voices like Stevie's are the rare pearl among the oysters. His voice on "Love Having You Around," "Superwoman," and "I Love Every Little Thing About You" is something otherworldly; it moves and digs and inspires in a way that any artist worth his salt, any music lover who adores the noise, would understand to be a gift. The same can be said for Donny Hathaway, with his butter-smooth delivery on songs like "A Song for You," "I Love You More Than You'll Ever Know," and "Someday We'll All Be Free," and Sly from Sly and the Family Stone, whose high-energy, leave-it-all-on-the-stage performance used to make people break out into a church-happy, "jogging for Jesus," hot, sweaty mass when he'd grab the mic. My job—indeed, my mission—as a singer and as an artist, was to build the perfect, distinctive, unique noise that would make my fans feel about my voice the way I do about Stevie's, Donny's, and Sly's. Let me keep it real: constructing that noise required, at first, some emulation.

Now, pulling this off isn't for amateurs. You can't just take someone else's vocals and claim them as your own without incurring the wrath. When I was a teenager singing around Tulsa, we played Stevie, Donny, and Sly's songs because they were Top 40 records and everybody loved to hear them. I'd kill them all. People would insist I sing Hathaway's "This Christmas" in the summertime. I mean, it'd be July 8 and they would have me singing it like Jesus was being born again that very night. But trust and believe, I would get called out when I sang a song exactly like Stevie or copied Donny's licks. My little brother, Robert, was good for this; he'd say loudly and harshly, "That's sounding too much like a Stevie Wonder riff." And so I'd change it up.

As I got more seasoned, I modified the recipe of my vocal stew by mixing different voices and styles together to help make my distinctive sound. Each of my favorite performers has a part in it. That roughness, that hardness, I get from Sly. That smoothness from Donny. Those licks, that's all Stevie. And the inflection, the mood I had in my throat already, is courtesy of my mom. As the years forged ahead, I hit my sweet spot on the mic, singing each of their essences out of my body. Every last one of their notes was balled up within me. Still, in order to be a star in my own right, I worked for years to craft that special Charlie Wilson sound.

When I asked God not to kill me out there on those streets, He heard my prayer but connected his blessing to something much deeper than what I was asking for. I wanted protection from the perils of addiction and homelessness. God granted that even more profoundly: He saved my voice and sound. Had my ability to sing a song and mean it gone away, surely I would have died.

Instead of diminishing the circle of influence—in terms of my voice—it opened doors for a new generation of singers who used my vocal style as a model to become formidable singers in their own right.

This was true even back when I was nearly homeless, depressed, and addicted. I was stumbling through the lobby of a fancy Beverly Hills hotel when, for the first time in my then-decades-long career, a big-shot music industry executive acknowledged that my voice was unique, revered, and iconic. This was sometime in the early nineties, right around the time that

The GAP Band wrestled itself away from our manager and each of us lost what little bit we had. I was on my way to my lowest, and Andre Harrell, who was founding Uptown Records, one of the most successful R & B and hip-hop labels of the nineties, was poised to make me feel, even if only for a moment, that I was worth a trillion bucks.

I didn't know who he was at first. When I walked through that hotel, I saw somebody at a long table with about thirty people sitting there eating, and when that guy raised his glass, the whole table raised theirs, too. It was quite a sight. I wanted to know who all those people were in there. When I walked in further to investigate, the man who made the toast yelled out, "Wait, hold up—stop the press! It's Charlie Wilson!"

He called me over. I wanted to sprint out the door. I wasn't in the best shape at that moment; I was strung out, didn't have a record deal or even a place to lay my head. But something made me walk over there. And when I got closer, I realized it was Andre with all of his artists at the table: Heavy D & the Boyz, Jodeci, Al B. Sure!, Teddy Riley and the hit nineties New Jack Swing group Guy, a host of others.

"I want to toast to Charlie Wilson, because it was your voice that made my label successful!" Andre boasted. He went on to say that he made every one of his artists listen to my voice—my vocal style—so that he could pattern his label off of it. I was blown away and much too taken aback to speak. The irony of my being literally penniless while he confessed he'd made his mint, in part, due to my voice wasn't lost on me.

"If you need anything, if there's anything I can do, just tell me," he added.

My mouth was wide open, but the words were stuck in my craw. I was too insecure to even pursue that line of dialogue. I didn't know how to talk to that man. I didn't know how to ask for what I wanted. I'd spent decades being ordered around, ripped off, threatened, and abused, being too trusting and too clueless about the industry to demand what was due me and my brothers, and now that I'd been stripped of everything I owned, my self-esteem offstage was about as vast as the wingspan of a flea. So rather than ask for Andre's help, I simply thanked him for the compliment and rushed out the hotel—back onto the streets. Back to . . . nothing.

You would think that the irony of it all would have made me angry. But it didn't. At that moment, that admission, those words, made me feel like I was somebody. As embarrassed as I was about the encounter, I did strut down that sidewalk, feeling richer than ever. I'll never forget that.

I was still getting high when I had the opportunity to work with Quincy Jones as a solo artist. He called me to do the song "Heaven's Girl" for his Grammy Award–winning album *Q's Jook Joint*, a song I was to record with R. Kelly, Ron Isley, and Aaron Hall from Guy. To say I was overjoyed by that call would be an understatement. When he reaches to play notes and all of these different arrangements and chord structures spring from his mind and his fingers, his music does for the ears what a mountainside of wild, colorful flowers does for the eyes. He is a genius.

Frankly, I was surprised he wanted to work with me, considering how he'd blown off The GAP Band way back in the day. Plus, through the years, I'd never heard from him for bigger collaborative projects, such as the time he produced "We Are the

World." In fact, The GAP Band never was asked to participate in big projects like that; all these incredible music moments were happening around us and we were left out. We thought the major producers didn't want to be bothered with us—chalked it up to the fact that we were stuck in a management situation that deterred professionals from reaching out to us. More, a small piece of me thought I wasn't worthy of their attention—that they didn't think I was a good enough singer, musician, or songwriter to tap for something bigger. It wasn't until much later that my brothers and I found out that Total Experience was blocking those blessings from us in their mad quest to keep total control over The GAP Band. I heard stories of opportunities that came our way but never happened.

For instance, there was one time when Kenneth "Babyface" Edmonds and LA Reid, who were being managed by SOLAR's Dick Griffey as part of the group the Deele, came to the studio looking for us. They wanted us to record a song they had written, and they came with cassette tape in hand for my brothers and me to hear it. When Lonnie came into the studio to let us know they were out in the lobby, he told us that we shouldn't go out to greet them because if we did, we'd cause problems for him with Griffey. "He might think I'm trying to steal the Deele from him," he said. "I don't want no trouble." The problem was that we believed Lonnie and took him at his word. Years later, LA told me that Lonnie greeted him and Babyface, offered to bring their cassette to us, and then left the duo sitting in the lobby for hours, only to go back out there and tell them that I had listened to their song and declared that they didn't know how to write! I'd see them from time to time and wonder why they'd never respond to my friendly hello. It was only when I finally confronted LA, who was in a convertible Bentley while I was in my homeless, raggedy way, that I put two and two together. I asked him point-blank why he never produced us.

"Really?" he asked.

"Really!" I said, defiant. I mean, they were hitting at the time; they had that song "Mary Mack," a record I loved, and I wanted to work with them.

"It never happened because that guy took our cassette and said that you said we couldn't write," LA said insistently.

"I said you couldn't write?" I asked. "Why would I say that? I never saw a cassette. I never heard a song!"

The single was "Rock Wit'cha," the monster hit that helped put Bobby Brown on the map after he left New Edition.

Something similar happened with Jimmy Jam and Terry Lewis, who I found out years later came to us with a few of those big songs Cherrelle recorded with Alexander O'Neal. We even missed out on a potential partnership with an old friend of ours, Roger Linn. He was the engineer for Leon Russell, and pulling on his talent and expertise, he designed the popular LM-1, the first programmable drum machine. We'd known that guy from when he was about sixteen or seventeen years old; he was a friend, and when we were all good and grown and making our mark on the industry, he came to the studio to talk to us about an exciting opportunity. We had no idea he was out in the lobby; he was left sitting out there for two hours. This would be like leaving the engineer for Beats By Dre sitting out on a bench for an ungodly amount of time. Dumb. When Roger's patience finally ran out, he left feeling disrespected and disgusted, but not before scribbling a note to me and my brothers: he wanted to tie The GAP Band to a new drum machine he'd developed with Akai, a Japanese electronics company that was about to make the young multimillionaire even more rich. When I understood what had happened, I confronted Lonnie.

"He was trying to disturb the shit," Lonnie said nonchalantly, like it wasn't a big deal.

"Disturb the shit?" I roared. "You see this fucking drum machine back here? He invented it!"

There were so many missed opportunities like that all through the nineties—opportunities that, even after things went bad with Total Experience, could have led to relationships with the biggest producers in the country, who could have kept our music going. We missed out on the big records but also, more important, the chance to make an even bigger mark on the industry. And that took its toll not only on our relationship as a group and as brothers, but on us as artists, especially for me as a singer who wanted, simply, to sing good songs. Being passed over and avoided and denied and ignored in this industry can be devastating.

This was in my heart the day I showed up for that session with Quincy Jones. Having not slept for ages, I looked like an addict when I went into the session, no question. When I saw Quincy, I said, "Man, do you know who I am?"

He said, "You gotta be kidding me, right? Of course I know who you are. Are you crazy?"

I told him that I wasn't sure because he'd never before called me to work with him on any of his projects. Plus, nobody wanted to be bothered with me because of the drugs. He must have detected I was down; he must have seen it in the way I carried myself in front of him, the way I was talking. In that moment, he softened up and told me a story about him back in the day that involved legendary jazz musician Charlie Parker, Ray Charles, and a few other music legends—a story that calmed my spirit. He said they were somewhere in France and Charlie Parker fell down the stairs and nobody could do anything about it because everybody was high. Quincy went on to say that when they went down to the bottom of the stairs, he was still alive, but there was a quick moment there when they thought they had lost him.

"From that moment on," he said, "I decided that somebody's gotta be sober and that somebody is going to be me." From that day forward, he insisted, he never touched another drug. "I had to be sober to make sure that I could watch everybody so that couldn't happen again. So you don't have to be afraid to be in here because I'm you and you are me."

Understanding that my addiction wasn't a revelation to him and that he understood the complex relationship between artists and their habits, I was a bit more at ease, and one would think that I would have wanted to embrace sobriety knowing that one of my musical heroes produced all that genius without the help of narcotics and elixirs. But that talk did nothing for my jones. I listened to him and held his gaze, but as soon as I walked out of the door, I went straight to the bathroom and took a couple hits.

I don't know if he knew I was high when I came back into that recording studio; if he did, he sure didn't show it. Instead, he continued to lift me up—to praise the one thing that no one but God could take from me. "Don't think about what people say about you: you are a true talent and a gift to this industry and this world. God gave you a gift and a talent. So don't listen to people and let them destroy your heart. You can sing!"

I sang my heart out for him on his iconic album *Q's Jook Joint*. The other guys—Aaron Hall and R. Kelly—weren't there, but I laid down my part for "Heaven's Girl," and then he asked me to sing on the remake of his signature song "Stuff Like That." I was supposed to do one song and I ended up doing four. He liked the way I worked; I had all these licks and runs that he loved and he said I was fast—like a rapper. "Boy, you're one take. 'One-Take Charlie'!" There was nothing cooler than that.

The next day, I was in a really bad way—too embarrassed to go back to the studio to meet up with R. Kelly and Aaron, who were there with Quincy, recording their parts. So I figured if I called over there and fooled around with them on the phone, the music would be all right and everyone would be happy. "What you doing?" I asked them over their speakerphone.

"Stealing your vocals!" R. Kelly said, laughing.

Sure enough, they mirrored all of the vocal inflections and ad-libs I'd recorded just the day before. If you listen closely to the way they're singing on that song, one is hard-pressed to distinguish their style of singing from mine.

Chapter 9

Getting Back to the Music

People always ask me how I feel about the younger guys such as K-Ci from Jodeci, Aaron Hall from Guy, and R. Kelly emulating my unique sound. It's become a staple question in almost every interview. Those journalists adjust their tape recorders and lean in, waiting for me to say I'm angry about it or offended. I'm not. Those men, each of them with their own unique talent, their own gift, honor me each time they sing. Their ability is God given; He molded their bodies in a fashion that allows them to create incredible sounds. And they have looked up to my voice as a model for how they can make beautiful music. And that's okay. I get it. Not just because with the help of my mother, Stevie, Donny, and Sly, I did it, too, but because I know what it means to grow up listening to someone and having their very existence as artists serve as the foundation for your own dreams. You have to remember, these guys who've emulated and collaborated with me—Andre Harrell, Teddy Riley, Jodeci, Aaron Hall, R. Kelly, Snoop Dogg, Kanye West, Justin Timberlake, Pharrell Williams, Master P, Mystikal—grew up listening to my music, just like I grew up listening to Stevie Wonder, Donny Hathaway, Sly, and the like. And it was that GAP Band sound and my voice and that of legends like Marvin Gaye and Curtis Mayfield and others with distinctive musical talents that the next generation of singers and musicians was grooving to when they were kids. It is only natural, then, that as they started articulating their own musical style, they colored their artistic expression with my vocal flair.

The GAP Band sound was distinctive, too. We were a synth-heavy funk group with a big mod funk sound—the kind that recalled Sly Stone and George Clinton and even Rick James. You have to remember that we were playing around the same time as other groups with very unique sounds and styles, such as Parliament Funkadelic, Earth, Wind and Fire, and Kool and the Gang, just to name a few. We were charged with creating our own sound and keeping it consistent from album to album. We needed to make sure that the first thing anyone heard musically sounded like a GAP Band song, whether you recognized it because of the drums or the guitar or my vocals. We aimed for that consistency. So we would always track everything out to really layer the sound of the records. For me, it started in the Moog bass effects pedal and then filtered into the beats. Of course, my brother had distinctive guitar chords and we would stack those. And then we would fuse that funk with a gospel sound and a bit of the blues. All of these contributed greatly to that GAP Band sound, which a generation of singers embraced and advanced.

Hearing people sing like me makes me feel good—like I did something to inspire somebody. Every last one of us in the music business wants to be a trailblazer. If we are not leaving something that somebody wants to emulate, then we haven't done our part. Granted, it took me some time to understand that I had this impact.

Interestingly, beyond the question of legacy, there is another benefit of having been so influential to a group of younger singers. Those artists who emulated my sound left the door open for me to reenter. Those younger, revered voices put my signature GAP Band licks on their popular contemporary R & B songs, thereby keeping the airwaves warm for me until I was able to make it back into the industry in a new, different way.

Little did I know that a call from Quincy would be the beginning of the next leg in my post-rehab musical journey. We recorded those songs for *Q's Jook Joint* in 1994 and by 1996, when I was well into my recovery, that monster album, a veritable staple on radio, had been nominated for seven Grammy Awards, including Best R & B Performance by a Duo or Group with Vocal for the song "Stomp!," to which I contributed. We did not win that particular Grammy, but my voice was blasting on speakers from New York to Compton, this time with deejays, music editors, and other R & B aficionados proclaiming me the "de facto father of New Jack Swing," the Teddy Riley–created genre that was buoyed by voices that sounded like mine: Aaron Hall, R. Kelly, K-Ci from Jodeci, and the like. I was excited— ecstatic, really—that people understood the significance of my contribution to music and loved the new work I was putting out.

All of this was happening just as Calvin "Snoop Dogg" Broadus was working on the follow-up to his huge debut album, *Doggystyle*, on Death Row Records and getting his own record label, Doggy Style Records, a subsidiary of Death Row, off the

ground. Almost at the same time as I was getting sober and starting my new life with Mahin, Snoop was in the fight of his life,
up on charges that he was involved in the death of a man shot
and killed by Snoop's bodyguard when he started Doggy Style.
Though his first album, produced by the legendary Dr. Dre, was
fueled by bass-and-keyboard–heavy funk samples, by the time
Snoop started his second album, he had a slightly different kind
of aesthetic in mind, one that incorporated that distinctive GAP
Band sound. And so he sent for me.

That was a huge step for him because Snoop was well aware
of my challenges. Indeed, he'd seen them firsthand one afternoon when he saw me on the streets of Hollywood, strung out,
with nowhere to go. On that fateful day, he was filling his gas
tank when he spotted me at the station, sitting on the side of the
building, no doubt nodding and high from whatever I was flying on. Years later, Snoop would tell me that he cried when he
realized who I was and reached in his pocket to float me some
money but then decided against it. "I wanted to give you some
money," he said, "but I didn't know if you were going to go get
high with it. You looked really, really bad. It hurt my heart."

When he heard me on the radio on Q's record and started
asking around about me, he did something much greater than
handing over a few dollars: Snoop put me on. He sent for me
through Val Young. Val had been a background singer for the
Brides of Funkenstein back in the late seventies and had already toured with Roy Ayers when The GAP Band hired her
as a background vocalist. That's her voice you hear mixed in "I
Don't Believe You Want to Get Up and Dance (Oops!)" and
on various songs on five of our albums. If you caught any of

our concerts in the eighties, she was right there on the stage with us. She was bad. After recording a couple of albums of her own—Rick James was her producer and she was signed to Mo-town—Val was still pretty plugged in to the music scene, touring as a backup singer and laying down background vocals with the likes of Bobby Brown, Miki Howard, Jimmy Jam and Terry Lewis, El DeBarge, Teddy Riley, and more, when she hooked up with Tupac to work on his song "To Live and Die in LA" on Death Row Records. I'm told she was in the studio bragging about how she knew me and had sung with The GAP Band when Snoop, who was down with Death Row at the time, asked her about me. "If you sing with Charlie Wilson, bring him to me," Snoop said insistently.

Val kept telling me that she was working with the rappers, but I wasn't paying her any mind. She liked to run her mouth; I'd just say, "Val, you know everybody," and move on to something else. Part of me didn't believe she really knew those guys; part of me wasn't really sure I was interested in dipping into that world.

I wasn't all that keen on joining in on yet another genre of music. After all, it wasn't like I was a hip-hop head or anything. I'd listened to Kurtis Blow and Run DMC and appreciated what they were doing musically. Hip-hop was taking over the music world and if you were listening to the radio, you had no other choice but to hear the records that were being played. What I appreciated more about the genre than the music itself was the artistry behind it; it was an expression, a movement, an un-apologetic manifestation of a culture that operated on the margins, in the shadows, in a completely different dimension from the staid music that celebrated fantasy, rather than the reality of the streets. It was very much in line with the way we were expressing ourselves in the funk genre; looking at it this way, it was only natural that Afrika Bambaataa would pay homage to George Clinton by performing in costumes that made him look like he'd just come in on the mother ship, or the Native Tongues would form a rap collective dedicated to uplifting a specific Afrocentric aesthetic that refused to conform, or that Dr. Dre would find his musical soul deep in the heart of the funk. But I didn't feel any burning need to be a part of it. I was heavy into R & B and pop.

On one particular day, however, Val, on a mission to connect me with Snoop, got smart: she skipped over my head and extended the invitation to Mahin. "You gotta bring him down to Can Am Studios," she said insistently. "Snoop wants to see him."

So with Val in one ear and Mahin in the other, I made it on down to that studio and sat in with Snoop on a session for a cut from his then-upcoming album *Tha Doggfather*. Our conversation was easy; I just started telling him my story, how far I'd gone, how low I'd sunk, how I had just started my sobriety journey, and how hard I was working to recover and get back into the game. He listened and expressed his support, and what's more, he understood how the havoc wreaked during my time at Total Experience affected me in so many ways because he had gone through similar challenges during his music career. As artists, we had something in common—a shared experience that made us protective of one another, of each other's art and heart. Snoop assured me that ours was going to be a solid relationship built on friendship, collaboration, and a mutual respect for good music. And then we got to work. I was deeply honored to be there.

Now, by this time, Dr. Dre had left Death Row and Snoop had DJ Pooh step in as the main producer making beats, very much in the same manner they'd done on *Doggystyle*, with live instrumentation of the songs they were sampling. That made me extremely valuable to Snoop and his creative vision, because he wanted to draw samples from GAP Band songs that my brothers and I had written, recorded, and performed. What I didn't want to do was hear our records chopped and screwed. James Brown, Parliament Funkadelic, The GAP Band—all of us had put it down and everybody had come along, taken our music, cut it up, and used it as their own, with zero nods given to the artistry that we'd cooked up. When James and a few other artists finally went to court over the blatant theft of their music, we felt a little better about the industry's take on sampling. Recognition. Credit. Cash. And so when I was in the room with Snoop, I felt better about the process. Plus, knowing that they were excited about tapping into our music for their sound felt good. If they didn't like it, they wouldn't have used it.

What Snoop and his producers didn't realize, though, is that I could actually play the music they wanted to sample—the GAP Band songs. And when I played them, he was just like, "Wow, we don't have to sample it!"

"That's right," I said.

I started playing the bass, the keyboards, and the guitar and recording some of the music, then humming different melodies and licks and parts for the other musicians and producers to play and lending all of myself—all of my talents—to the creation of something beautiful. He and his producers put that hip-hop flavor to it to make it a modern, smoothed-out G-funk sound. Snoop seemed to be blown away by the fact that my voice was still strong and that I could play so many instruments. "Man, you can still sing," he said in that slow, silky Compton drawl. "GAP's in play. That's a true musician right there."

"Yeah, man." I smiled. "I can still sing, and play, too."

It was something else to be a musician in the room again—to participate in the art of collaboration. About a year earlier, my addiction had me convinced I wouldn't ever play again. That the music in me was gone. Not long into the process, we came up with "Snoop's Upside Ya Head," a take on The GAP Band's "Oops Up Side Your Head," with that distinctive Charlie Wilson sound. This was only right because, really, if it doesn't sound like Charlie Wilson, why would you bother to have me there? Snoop valued that, plus he had respect for me not only as an artist but as an elder. I mean, let's be honest: Snoop's lyrics on *Doggystyle* were lewd—shocking. And I was uncomfortable with the idea of contributing my talents to music that was so unapologetically explicit and misogynistic. Snoop toned it down. That earned him quite a bit of flak from Tupac, who proclaimed Snoop "soft" for hanging around with "Uncle Charlie." But he was able to make some quality product with just as much of a musical impact without being as salacious as he was on his first album, and I'm proud of him for that.

I did a few sessions with Nate Dogg when I started collaborating with Snoop. I would write hooks and sing melodies, while Nate sat in the corner with his pencil and paper, asking, "Where's the hook?" Our collaboration was just . . . different. I didn't sit around waiting for Snoop to tell me what he wanted; we worked together, exchanging ideas and following each other's rhythms to create music *together*. And I think Snoop appreciated that about my work. When he finally extracted himself from Death Row—he was upset and quite vocal about the fact that he didn't think Suge Knight was giving him, one of the biggest stars of the label, the kind of money, power, and respect he deserved, plus Suge was doing a stint in prison—Snoop found his way to Master P's No Limit Records in Louisiana, and brought me with him as his collaborator. As a result, I was introduced to and played with a whole new arena of rappers who also wanted to make good music with a veteran. I recorded with Mystikal, Mia X, and a few other rappers down in Baton Rouge, a venture that proved lucrative for this artist, who'd spent a lifetime being famous but having little to show for it. Master P took good care of me; I'd record something and he'd catch up to me and hand me a stack of bills and say, simply, "Here, man, go take your wife shopping." That was the way of the rapper's world.

Of course, navigating the hip-hop domain had its challenges. Most of the men who were at the top of their game at the time understood that when it came to business, there was no room for old street habits in the industry's boardrooms. The last thing on their mind was gangbanging, gun toting, and bringing someone else harm; money—real money—was made when they focused, instead, on making hits. Still, controlling the circle of people around them, guys who came from the old neighborhood wearing their gangsta ways on their chests like platinum badges of honor, was no easy feat, and sometimes the behavior of the streets found its way into the heart of our work spaces.

Such was the case one afternoon when I was recording at Master P's No Limit studios in New Orleans. He was unapologetically strict about keeping street elements far away from his business; he was a legitimate music mogul and maintained a zero-tolerance policy for guns, drugs, fighting, and the like anywhere around him. Still, trouble found my wife and me while I was recording for one of his artists. The studio was small—so much so that Mahin had to sit out in the hallway while I worked. Now, normally I wouldn't leave my wife sitting out in a hallway, but because there were already three other people in our tiny work space, we had no other choice but to be separated. While she sat, two guys came into the space and started talking; one suddenly pulled out a gun and started fooling around with it, cocking and cleaning it, without any regard for Master P's rule or who saw him. And then, suddenly, the gun went off—right there in that tiny waiting area, where my wife was sitting, waiting patiently for me. That bullet, which the shooter didn't realize was in the chamber, went straight past my wife's ear and lodged itself in the wall, aligned just slightly to the right of her head.

"I'm so sorry, ma'am," the man yelled. "Oh my God, I'm so sorry. I didn't mean to do that."

Within moments, a crowd of dudes was standing over the culprit, calling him everything but a child of God. They snatched that gun out of his hands and started beating him. Had Master P been there, I have no doubt that he would have been stomped to death.

"Don't tell Percy!" he begged as he took his licks. "Don't tell Master P!"

"Man, if he finds out you brought a gun in here and you almost killed Charlie Wilson's wife? You're done!" one guy said, seething.

With that, the gunman took off running. I can't say I blame him. Master P had a policy that if ever anyone in his crew caused a problem, he would make them put on boxing gloves and spar with him. A beating was practically guaranteed, as Master P was a helluva boxer who could swing with the best of them. If you couldn't fight, he would just keep beating you with those boxing gloves until you couldn't take it anymore.

I knew then not to tell him that my wife could have died that afternoon. I implored everyone in the room to keep it quiet. These guys, hard dudes from the streets of New Orleans, did not have to listen to me, but they did. Perhaps it was because they knew that their friend would suffer serious repercussions. Maybe they thought they, too, would get in trouble, just for being there. I'd like to think, though, that they listened to me because they respected my authority, my wisdom. I have that kind of connection to the younger generation. When I am there, I am Uncle Charlie. When I walk into the room, the hardest guy, with a gun at his waist, a criminal record that spans the length of my arm, and a glass eye he got after losing his real one in a prison-yard fight, will stop midpunch to greet me. It'll be, "Wait, hold up! Uncle Charlie is in this mug. That's Uncle Charlie right there! Let me get a picture with you right quick!" There have been times when fights have literally broken out in the studio in front of me and Mahin, and afterward, someone will come over and apologize, saying, "I'm so sorry, Uncle Charlie and Ms. Wilson. We didn't mean for that to go down in front of you."

Snoop and I, especially, had good times together. One of my most memorable experiences on the road with him was our 1997 trip to perform at Lollapalooza. Snoop had two buses, but nobody wanted to ride with me because I didn't allow drinking or smoking on our bus. Everybody was on Snoop's bus, partying, and on our bus, the one I shared with Mahin and her son, Michael Paran, who was helping his mom with management duties on my behalf, you could hear crickets. Still, we had our fun, performing for an amazing audience—a diverse crowd the likes of which I hadn't seen since my days traveling with Leon Russell, the Rolling Stones, and Kiss. The trip almost was marred by one particularly racist incident, when we stopped at a restaurant in Utah to get food. I was incredibly tired, so I stayed on the bus while Michael and Mahin went in to sit and eat and order some takeout for me. The waitress thought nothing of seating the two at a table and handing them menus, but when Snoop's brother Jerry joined them, she became repulsed.

"You have to leave," she sneered, snatching the menus from the table and glaring at Jerry.

"What are you talking about? We'd like to order dinner," Mahin said insistently.

"We have the right not to serve you," the waitress said, undeterred. "You have to go."

Though there were no "whites only" signs hanging above the door, apparently it was against restaurant policy, in 1997, to serve black people at this particular establishment.

Disgusted, my wife, who is Persian, went to a nearby store where some of the band members were to tell them what happened; the cashier, overhearing the story, informed Mahin that the convenience store, too, was owned by the same person as the restaurant.

Mahin reached out and grabbed the hand of a band member, who had just laid a few goodies on the counter by the register. "Don't you buy a thing in here," she said. "They are racist and don't deserve your money."

"Okay, Little Mommy," he said simply, calling her by the nickname Snoop and his people had bestowed on my wife.

Ten minutes later, that same band member climbed up onto our tour bus bearing cookies from the convenience store. Mahin was hot. "I told you not to buy anything from there!" she yelled.

"Oh, don't worry," he said, ripping open his own pack of cookies. "I didn't spend any money in there."

The entire bus fell out in laughter. "Oh, you told the wrong person that," Snoop said, chuckling.

Indeed.

. . .

While I was building up my catalog as the voice behind some of hip-hop's hottest artists, The GAP Band was finally realizing a financial reward for our hard work. We have Mahin's son, Michael, to thank for this. A smart young law student at the time, he had some fine ideas for how The GAP Band could get back to what we did best. One night, after a gig at The Strand in Redondo Beach, California, he came backstage and I asked him to count out our money and divvy it up between us brothers. He was sitting in the middle of the floor, sorting out bills, when I literally heard someone say in my ear, "Hire him." I looked behind me, but no one was there. God was talking to me again.

So I said to no one in particular, "Wow, I heard somebody say, 'Hire him.'" I called everybody in the room together and I said, "From this day forward this guy, Michael Paran, is going to manage us."

Michael looked up from counting the money, looked around the room and then back at me, and said, "Who, me?"

"Yeah, you're going to be our manager."

Michael accepted the job and hit the ground running: he read books, learned all about the business of music, went through all the contracts we'd had, and, with tears in his eyes, said, "I promise you, I will never, ever let anyone take advantage of you ever again." For two years, he worked and didn't pay himself. He made sure that The GAP Band got everything: the right prices, better venues. He even went toe-to-toe with crooked concert promoters who, knowing our tenuous touring and recording history, made a point of trying to take advantage of us. There were many times he would seek them out to collect our performance money and they would threaten him and refuse to hand over the cash. He was young then, with a huge heart, but neither of those traits meant he was stupid. Indeed, he was the mastermind behind the funk supergroup United We Funk, consisting of The GAP Band, Zapp and Roger, the SOS Band, Dazz Band, the Bar-Kays, Con Funk Shun, Rick James, and the Ohio Players, and had us touring nationally for two years, setting the standard for many of the multiact tours today. Even in the middle of all of that action—especially so—he had our back. Like the time when we had a show with Zapp and Cameo, and just before we were about to head to the stage, the promoter told Michael he didn't have our money, but he could pay with a personal check.

"They're not going on that stage unless you pay them," Michael said insistently, advocating hard for us.

Eyes wide, the sound of a full house ringing in his ears, the promoter backed off his ploy and reached down into his pocket, producing a credit card. "This has enough money on it to pay the fellas to perform," he said, seething.

After a couple of phone calls to check the credit card balance, Michael was convinced the promoter could cover our pay and only let us take the stage once he ran the credit card and our cash was in hand. Later that night, the managers behind Zapp and Cameo expressed shock that Michael had gotten our money, because that same promoter had stiffed them. Michael felt so bad about that that he gave Zapp money out of his own pocket for gas for the group's tour bus and for food. That's the kind of guy Michael Paran is. He made a point of winning. For us. And with his support, direction, dedication, and love, we started making decent money, then good money, then big money. We could all finally afford our own homes and cars, with a little money left over. Robert even had Michael save some of his money for him. It was incredible. Finally, The GAP Band was reaping the rewards of our musical talent. And my voice, the instrument that God protected while I was out there on those streets, was doing for me what I could never accomplish while working with Total Experience: it was providing a way. I have Snoop and Michael to thank for that breakthrough.

Chapter 10

Snoop

It was Calvin Broadus Jr.—you know him as the rapper Snoop Dogg—who announced me to the world as "Uncle Charlie." But the title wasn't some rap moniker or gimmicky nickname, and it sure wasn't meant as the insulting reference racists used to lob at older black men back in the day; Snoop called me "Uncle" out of admiration and respect for our friendship. Indeed, because we are family.

In the beginning, ours was an easy bond. Those initial sessions in the studio, when he was taking his first steps away from Death Row Records and I was piecing myself together both personally and musically, were filled with moments of admiration for each other's skills. Snoop's abilities as a rapper, soft-spoken and smooth and steeped in the very essence of G-funk, were something to behold; his voice was like the buttery rap answer to the soulful, velvety stylings of Al Green, with a laser-sharp focus on the reality of black lives that mirrored what Marvin Gaye was hitting with *What's Going On*, or what I loved about Curtis Mayfield's lyrical observations on sociopolitical and pop cultural moments that helped to ignite the passions of a people in the sixties. With that easy-like-Sunday-morning Southern twang dancing up and through his words, Snoop was making poetic what it was like to live on the streets of Long Beach—a collage of gangster, pimp, and drug experiences that captured what I was seeing while I was homeless and addicted, tottering from stash houses to rooms overrun with the illegal narcotics and the sex trade that made up that world's underbelly. He wasn't rapping; he was kicking game—laid-back but still very much in control. I liked that about his artistry—about him.

As for Snoop, he seemed genuinely enamored with my musical abilities—and with me. In those first few days of our working together, he would entertain me with stories about being raised in a house where funk lived. He would lie at his mother's feet, listening to Parliament Funkadelic and Sly and the Family Stone, Kool and the Gang and Earth, Wind and Fire, and, of course, The GAP Band, learning about the stylings from his mom and letting the instrumentation, melodies, and lyrics seep into his bones. "I listened to you all's music because my mama played all of that," he told me easily. "I learned about you from my mom."

But he would learn a lot more about me outside of the music, when we moved on from being musical colleagues and started getting to know each other as men. Those deeper conversations—about family, loyalty, love, fatherhood, how to do right—came slowly at first, then opened up like floodgates once I started hanging with him and his family outside the studio, back at his home. His babies were really little then, and they

called me Uncle Charlie. Snoop joined in after I started school-
ing him on the ways of men and talking to him like a father.
I would talk to him about how to have a relationship with his
wife, how to be a good father to his children, how to simply
be. In that advice were lessons—all the things I'd learned from
my own trials, tribulations, and triumphs as a husband, father,
and artist. "You don't want to make the same mistakes I did," I'd
warn him.

Snoop wasn't rebellious when it came to the advice I gave
him; generally, he listened to what I had to say and even took my
advice. But in the beginning, he was taken aback when I started
talking to him about making changes in his life—changes in the
way he did business, the way that he presented himself as an artist, the way he cared for his body, the way he loved his wife and
their family. My wife and I talked to him about everything. We
were muscling him so hard on every little thing that every once
in a while he would kind of look at me sideways and say, "Man,
nobody tells me anything about my house and what I'm supposed to do with it. Every time I make a move, here y'all come."
Truly, we were like parents to him, and he was our hardheaded
but loved son.

One time I went in there preaching about his weed habit.
He's never made a secret of his love for marijuana. In interviews,
pictures, his lyrics, and his videos, Snoop espouses the virtues
of smoking and portrays himself as one of the most vocal pro-
ponents of the drug. Spend more than five minutes around him
and it's clear he loves the stuff. But when we started working together, the life he was getting from inhaling was killing me. My
wife was the first one to say something about it; she didn't waste

any time getting right down to it, either. On the first day I took her to the studio, she laid down Mahin's Law. She has an accent and she struggles with the letter S, so she ends up putting "uh" in front of it, which made the way she called Snoop's name interesting enough. But what she said made Snoop snap to attention. "Uh-Snoop," she demanded, "y'all can't uh-smoke and get high around my husband. He's recovering."

"Word?" he said, clearly taken aback by the request.

That was the first day we met; I'll never forget that. He turned to his boys, who were in the studio smoking with him, and said, "Okay, y'all gotta put this out. Charlie Wilson is coming in here." He took her request that he stop smoking around me under advisement and respected what she had to say about it as a former drug counselor who had seen up close the downward spiral an addict could take simply by being around people who were drinking or doing drugs. She was afraid that his habit, and particularly his penchant for smoking in the studio while he was working, would trigger a relapse for me.

Of course, I was concerned about that, too, even years into my recovery, but I was equally worried that he would fall prey to the same demons that tried to take me out when I was addicted and being robbed, abused, and taken advantage of by the predators who'd been surrounding me. So one day when I was visiting his house, I spoke up and told him he'd have to quit it. And when I tell you I went in? I mean, I went *in*. I pulled him into his kitchen and let it fly. "Man, I can't stop you from doing what you're doing, but I can't be around that weed because I'm a recovering alcoholic and addict, and the way you're around here smoking, you're no different from a crackhead as far as I'm concerned," I said. "Shit, look at y'all. You're talking about how you saw me that time at the gas station, high and looking all bad and everything, but I'm looking at you, and you can't even cut a damn song because you're too high to get the work done. You're in there laughing and giggling and too high to do what you're supposed to be doing.

"Let me tell you this, man," I said, "I really love you. You've got a beautiful wife, you got these kids, and I know there's a lot of craziness going on in here, but you're going to have to quit smoking weed."

"What?" he asked, clearly taken aback. "For real?"

"Man, you're going to have to quit. You're smoking and smoking and smoking, and what good is it doing you? Come on, man!"

I talked to him nonstop for a good ten minutes. When I finally stopped talking, he was quiet for a good half a minute as he stared at me with this look, as if to say, "Man, who the hell do you think you are?" But when he finally spoke, I was shocked by what he had to say.

"Okay," he said. "All right. I'm going to stop."

You could have knocked me flat on my behind. I'd expected a fight. Or for him to lay me out. But instead, he listened to me— actually took my advice and quit smoking weed right at that very moment.

Admittedly, I didn't fully believe he was going to do what he said, but he did. The next day, I asked his wife, Shante, how he was doing and she was shocked. "He hasn't smoked," she said. "What did you say to him, Uncle Charlie?"

That day without smoking turned into a week for Snoop,

then it turned into two weeks, and then a month and then another month, and then he sent out an official message into the industry saying that he'd quit smoking. Honestly? I couldn't believe he'd listened. I know that he faced an enormous amount of pressure behind the decision; people would go over to his house with weed and he was trying to keep people away from his door. "They keep coming, Uncle Charlie," he complained.

I told him I knew it better than most, as the same thing happened to me. I offered to sic Mahin on them but he said he could handle it himself and he did. Snoop, the self-proclaimed weed connoisseur, quit smoking for almost a year.

I continued to counsel him on various things, one area of which was marriage. I reminded him, for instance, that he and his wife made a commitment to each other and that the key to his success was in the bond he created with his wife and children. I needed him to listen to and respect what I was saying to him as a man, and thankfully, he did, because really, he's been famous almost as long as not and he was used to people doing what he said, catering to his every demand and, at home, being the man of his house.

"Nobody's ever tried to talk to me like this, man. Never," he said with joyful tears in his eyes. He went on to tell me that he'd missed having a true father figure in his life while he was growing up—how his stepfather divorced his mother when he was just four and how his biological father hadn't come back into his life until after he became a superstar. "I had nobody, man. I grew up in the hood, just me and my mama. But you're teaching me a lot right now."

I was proud of Snoop and Shante for working hard to make

their marriage last, so much so that I debuted "There Goes My Baby," a fan-favorite song about the first time a man meets and falls in love with his woman, at their vow-renewal ceremony, which they held at my ranch. The song has an old feel to it, but the lyrics are modern, fresh, and tell a story that I just knew the two of them could relate to. They loved it—everyone did—and I was pleased about that. But I was even more honored to feature them in the song's video as a visual testament to Snoop's love for his wife. It was Michael Paran's idea to gather footage from Snoop and Shante's wedding and other special moments in their lives and put it together in a documentary-style illustration of the song, and I couldn't have been more happy to do so. The twinkle in their smiles, the tears in Snoop's eyes, the way the two of them embrace, the way their kids look at them with admiration, all of that makes my heart swell.

I had more advice: "Let your wife run the business. Let her be a part of your organization. Let her be with you. You're gone for five and six and seven days at a time, and though she knows you're somewhere in Germany, she really doesn't know where you are. All she wants is to be with you. You're her family. She's your family. Family sticks together."

He finally did listen to that; his wife is involved in his business, though he and Shante categorically refuse to be around each other every day all day, like me and Mahin. I brought that up and both of them looked at me as if I were crazy and said, practically simultaneously, "I don't know if we can do all that, Uncle Charlie!" We laughed so hard we all fell out.

Chapter 11

Going Solo

My father could see it plain as day. He had the gift of sight, which he used back when he left Tulsa as a young boy and found himself preaching in that dark, expansive field, miles away from home. Somewhere in the recesses of his mind, the picture was stark and highlighted in Technicolor, and Dad couldn't keep the image to himself any longer. "Son," he said, putting his hand on my shoulder one night after a GAP Band concert in California, "you need to get going."

"What do you mean?" I asked, toweling myself off, the sweat and funk of my work onstage pouring from my body. As had been usual over the few years leading up to that very moment, my father was backstage waiting in the wings for his sons after our show, a practice he started after The GAP Band got really big and we were selling out shows and such. Though we agreed to take him on the road with us, initially I was still bitter—mad as hell, really—about his leaving our family. Leaving me. My older brother was the first one to forgive him, then my sister, followed by my little brother. But it wasn't until I got much older and we were able to talk like men about the kind of father he was to me that I could truly understand my dad's absence. I never could support his ability to cut off things—romantic relationships, work, especially his family—and keep on moving, but when I finally let go of the anger and opened my eyes to who my father truly was, I came to know him as a good preacher and a good man capable of emotion, capable of love. Capable of loving me, his son. And I could give him that love in return. As we grew close, he grew to love Mahin, too, and often called her his favorite daughter-in-law. Just as Snoop learned in time to be open to what I had to say, I respected what my father had to say.

"I'm telling you, you need to get going," my father told me that night backstage. "But this door is closing quickly. You need to go and don't look back."

"But, Dad, what about—"

"Son, don't look back at none of this," he said insistently. "It's time for you to go out on your own. This GAP Band door is closing and I've already seen something for you. But, Charles, son, you need to go now, quickly, or you're going to miss out."

He was right, and one didn't need the gift of sight to see that. Things hadn't been right between my brothers and me for years, and though we were out of the clutches of Total Experience and finally making good money under Michael Paran's management and direction, there were serious fissures in our working relationship. My brothers seemed to think that I had hired Michael for my own benefit—that he was there solely to make sure that my career soared, sans The GAP Band. This couldn't have been further from the truth: I hired Michael because I wanted to be represented by somebody who could help us make money. Rather than embrace Michael as our manager, my brothers set about trying to break him. Every interaction was a battle. An example: it seemed that while we were touring, we could hardly make it off the tour bus and into hotels before my brothers would head into the lobby, pining for a fight. "What do you mean, the room doesn't have my name on it?" one would be yelling, confronting the hotel staff about our rooms. Mind you, Michael would have just told everyone back at the bus to wait while he got everything situated, and that he would be back shortly with room keys. This was the professional way of getting things done. I understood why my brothers acted this way: in the past, they and I were so busy getting high that abiding by rules and moving through the music world in a professional manner were completely foreign. It was nothing to have friends and family hanging out on the stage while we were performing, or for us to simply behave irresponsibly in front of the concert promoters who were charged with paying us at the end of the night. Michael's mission was to do away with that unprofessionalism we exhibited in our earlier iteration, so that the people who were working with us now could see that we'd cleaned up our act and that we deserved to get the pay, recognition, and respect worthy of a group of our stature.

Still, my brothers remained unimpressed. One night, this became all too clear when we attended a business meeting to make a deal for The GAP Band and Ronnie showed up with D. J. Rogers, our old label mate from Total Experience Records. Before the two of them could sit in their chairs, Ronnie said: "D. J. is going to be my manager." Just like that. With a smug look on his face as if nothing else we had to say, nothing else Michael had done for all of us, mattered. Needless to say, I was shocked. Michael was hurt. Months later, Ronnie started calling Michael his manager again, but the damage had been done.

We had already missed out on some writer's fees and publishing royalties for all of those iconic GAP Band songs that we had written and that still play on the radio to this day. But out on the road, we were free to do what we loved—sing and perform—and get paid for it. That was where the money was—it was our livelihood—and Michael saw to it that we went from small, to decent, to mid-great, to great numbers on tour. Still, my brothers did not trust him. Michael did everything he humanly could do to be transparent with them, down to showing them something as mundane as how much he saved seeking out discounted airfare for trips to tour venues. After all we'd been through, Michael was going above and beyond to try to show his value, to prove he was a great manager. But my brothers wouldn't cut Michael a break. And that irked me, because I never once heard either of them say, "Let me see the books," when others managed us. I knew that my signing us to Total Experience had hurt us, but I did the best I could, given how little I knew about the business side of the industry. This time around, I was telling them that hiring Michael was me grabbing the bull by the horns and making sure that we were getting money and getting paid, but they weren't hearing it.

Michael was bearing the brunt of it at first, but soon, it interfered with our interactions with one another. It was particularly acute backstage, where my wife would join me. I'd insisted that we have separate dressing rooms, not because I didn't want to be with my brothers, but because everybody would be getting into costumes, naked between changes and such. I didn't want Mahin, who went everywhere with me, around all of that, so I would make sure we had a private space. But my request for a private dressing room rubbed them the wrong way. There were other nights when we would all come off the stage and my brothers would take the car back to the hotel, leaving me at the venue. There I'd be, sweat-soaked and worn out, stuck in the dressing room with no way to get back to where we were staying, time and time again.

If I had to hazard a guess as to what came between us, I'd say that they were afraid that Michael was secretly working solely for my benefit and not for the collective. But I had never once said, "We're Charlie Wilson and The GAP Band," and I wasn't about to start at almost fifty years old. I rode hard for The GAP Band, but I never got the sense in our last days together as a group that the feeling was mutual, as uncomfortable as it is to admit.

For example: I did a solo album—my second—in 2000, an independent venture with the record label Major Hits Records. The label was financed by a man who amassed his fortune during the technology boom in the early 2000s; he was a big fan of soul music and looking for ways to invest in the genre when a member of my team introduced Michael and me to him. He took a liking to me, my music, and my vision and agreed to give us the seed money we needed to produce my own project, my way. With that capital, Michael hired a team—production, marketing, publicity, the works—and we set about creating, from the ground up, an album that showcased not only my ability to make good music but my willingness to place all my bets on *me.* That major record labels refused to believe in my work did not matter. What mattered is that I believed in myself and was mostly surrounded by people who shared in that vision.

We worked hard, too: there was no difference between what our label did for me and what a major label does for its own artists. We did and paid for everything: studio time, songwriters and producers, distribution fees, marketing, a team of people who were responsible for getting buy-in from radio stations across the country.

That album, called *Bridging the Gap*, debuted on the Top 200 *Billboard* chart and managed to yield the hit single "Without You," a beautiful ballad that climbed to number one on *Billboard*'s Adult R&B chart—my first number one single as a solo artist. Music television stations also gave a lot of airtime to the song and seemed to really dig its beautiful, spare video, which reintroduced me to fans in a much more pared-down, modern way. We cultivated an image that was vastly different from the funk cowboy look I'd long been known for as part of The GAP Band. Back when releasing independent albums was considered taboo in an industry that prided itself on handpicking and force-feeding stars and hits to consumers, I broke through the barrier and created my own platform on which to stand as Charlie Wilson, solo artist.

The success of my album was buoyed by a genius idea that Michael brought to the table: I would become a featured star in small but popular plays traveling to urban areas throughout the country. Of course, when the idea was proposed, people couldn't see the vision: why on earth would Charlie Wilson sing and act on what is commonly referred to as "the Chitlin' Circuit"? For me, the answer was as obvious as a signature "ooooh weeeee" on a Charlie Wilson song: those plays drew sizable audiences in all the markets where we were counting on *Bridging the Gap* being successful: Atlanta, Detroit, Chicago, New York, Cleveland, and the like. In any given city, thousands of people would come see me act and sing "Outstanding" and "Without You" in a wholesome show full of great storytelling and performances and then they'd wake up to my song on the same adult urban radio stations that promoted the plays. This was the sweet spot. That's the audience I could count on to support my work. And they did.

Not to mention, appearing in those plays did wonders for putting me back on a sound financial footing. At the time, performing with The GAP Band was still a cut-rate proposition, with modest performance fees being split three different ways between my brothers and me after expenses. Michael was able to negotiate much more lucrative deals with the playwrights and theater promoters, who were pulling in crowds of three thousand people at least four times a week when they toured a show. It wasn't rocket science.

In my mind, I'd envisioned being Charlie Wilson the solo artist as well as Charlie Wilson the lead singer of The GAP Band. But no one else, it seemed, was on board with my plans— not the concert promoters, not the booking agents, and especially not my brothers. Whenever I would try to get shows on my own, the first question I'd inevitably get from the promoters was, "You're going to do GAP Band songs, right?" And when I booked shows with my brothers, no one wanted to give me the spotlight so I could play and sing my songs. They especially weren't interested in hearing about a "GAP Band featuring Charlie Wilson" tour. My brothers were really clear: "We're not doing 'featuring Charlie Wilson' nothing," they said. Ronnie was also upset because he had been performing in urban plays as well. With two Wilson brothers to choose from, promoters were more inclined to hire the lead singer of The GAP Band—me. Those plays would go for eight weeks at a time, but I would still have ten months out of the year touring as part of The GAP Band, and all that time, there was tension. It got ugly.

The dissension was unbearable and soon, things fell apart. That was when I made one of the toughest decisions of my career: I left The GAP Band to pursue a full-on solo career.

For decades, my brothers and I had performed, approaching the stage and recording like a battalion of soldiers going to war together. But now I was going to be the lone sniper—out there by myself. The pressure was huge. I was anxious about what was to come. But I knew I had to forge ahead, this time, on my own.

Chapter 12

Charlie, Last Name Wilson

I owe my huge solo breakthrough to R. Kelly, the singer, song-writer, and producer recognized in the industry as one of the most successful artists in the US and the creator of monster hits like "I Believe I Can Fly" and Michael Jackson's "You Are Not Alone." We'd been talking for a while about doing some records but he sort of disappeared for a couple years while he created and produced the "Mr. Biggs" project with Ron Isley of the Isley Brothers. For that project, R. Kelly produced an epic saga of drama, love, betrayal, and retribution between a mob boss (Mr. Biggs, as portrayed by Ron Isley) and his security guard (R. Kelly), played out in top-charting songs and large-budget, glossy videos that saturated the radio airwaves and music television shows during its heyday. In other words, R. Kelly was busy; our partnership didn't pan out. But when I finally decided to make a full go of being a solo artist, I went on a mission to get a song from R. Kelly.

I tracked him down in Chicago, while I was performing in a play. A guy named Deon, who'd been charged with driving me and my wife around while I was in town to perform, said he knew where R. Kelly would be playing basketball that night. "Take me there," I said.

We arrived at the gym, a small, private sports center somewhere deep in the hood, and an hour passed. No R. Kelly. Two hours, no R. Kelly. My wife was looking at me sideways because I was sitting in this random gym in the hood in Chicago, with all this jewelry on and a bunch of money in my pocket, and there's no sign of R. Kelly or anyone else we knew, for that matter. Mahin, who had her purse full of my night's earnings, thought for sure that we were being set up, and she said so. Several times. We were, after all, perfect targets for a robbery, especially at three a.m. in Chi-town. So I finally made my move and told Deon we were ready to go.

"No, don't leave—he's here. He just pulled up," Deon said insistently before walking away.

I looked at Mahin and she looked at me right back. "Man," I said. "We're about to get robbed."

Another hour passed before he finally walked into the gym. Mahin and I had just finished staking out a way to escape quickly in case anything popped off, when Deon walked up to a man I didn't recognize and pointed us out to him. That man walked over and looked me up and down. Because I had on sunglasses and a hat, he didn't realize who I was at first, so he shrugged and walked away. He went back out onto the court and played two games before taking a seat on the bench to adjust his sneakers. That's when I went to him and took off my shades.

"Oh man—Uncle Charlie!" he said, hugging me. "What you doing here?"

"I'm here trying to find out why you lied to me all these years about producing a record for me," I said, only half joking.

"Aw man—here we go," he said easily. "What you doing here in Chicago anyway?"

"I'm doing a play," I said.

"A play?" R. Kelly asked. "I've never been to a play."

I invited him to my play and he attended; later, we went back to the hotel and then to the studio, where he listened to some of my music and watched me interact with the crew that was help-ing me record my album. He came to the play the next night, too, with Ron Isley in tow. After my performance, the three of us headed over to the studio, where Ron talked so much, R. Kelly actually fell asleep on the both of us. But when he opened his eyes again, he popped up with a pitch.

"I got the idea for this song," he said.

"What's the idea?" I said.

"Okay, so Mr. Biggs goes to prison and he's in Colombia, right? Then you go to prison, too, and Mr. Biggs busts out of jail and then he comes back to get you and you get on his private jet, take all his women, and leave him—"

I cut him off right there. "This is about to turn into some kind of cliché," I said. "I'm not really feeling that. I don't want to do a record like that." I had already made a mess of my career once and was working hard to recover from that. The last thing I wanted to be was somebody's gimmick.

R. Kelly got quiet and plunged deep into thought. "Okay," he said finally, "there has to be a way to reintroduce you."

"Yeah," I said. "I'm just Charlie Wilson. How we going to do that?"

"Yeah, that's right," he said. "Charlie Wilson."

With that on his mind, R. Kelly left to go play basketball and, in the wee hours of the morning, met me at the studio. "I got something for you," he said excitedly as he rushed in. He sat down at the keyboards and played this slow, spare melody and sang the beginnings of his song, "Charlie, Last Name Wilson." I started laughing when I heard it (that little laugh is still on the record). R. Kelly is a genius, an incredible songwriter and artist.

"Man, I can just reintroduce you as your own name!" he said.

"Yeah," I said in agreement. "Reintroduce me. I don't want to be anybody else—not Mr. C, not Mr. Bob. I want to use my own name. Charlie Wilson. First name Charlie, last name Wilson."

That was something we used to say back home in Tulsa when we were staking our claim and puffing out our chests. It would go like this: "You know who I am, don't you? First name Charlie, last name Wilson." We would say that to each other with all this bravado, all the while falling with laughter. I don't know if he used to say that around his way, but R. Kelly sure nailed the sentiment on so many levels with that song, which would eventually become my first monster solo single, "Charlie, Last Name Wilson." He came up with a record that would reintroduce me to the world—not by calling me out of my name or creating some Mr. Biggs–esque persona that had nothing to do with who I really am as a person. Buoyed by the success of that single and the work of other great songwriters and producers such as will.i.am, Justin Timberlake, the Underdogs, and the Platinum Brothers, my album *Charlie, Last Name Wilson* debuted at number ten on the *Billboard* Top 200 chart and was certified gold after selling more than five hundred thousand copies. I had a solo hit on my hands.

Thing is, the music business is such a tricky affair. A chart-topping comeback success story doesn't necessarily translate into respect from the people who hold your career in their hands, and this is especially true when you fall outside the mold the industry equates with success: I came into a full-on solo career in my fifties, in the wake of a defunct funk band, and sans controversy or any ability or desire to rap. In other words, at the time I made my splash, I was not an obvious star.

In some ways, my record company didn't see it, either. Though the label was supportive of *Charlie, Last Name Wilson*, the label execs didn't think a second album could succeed without R. Kelly, and so they insisted that they would only pay for, support, and distribute a second Charlie Wilson album if R. Kelly produced it. I was open to the idea, but this was no easy proposition, considering R. Kelly was going through his own problems and scandals and did not make it a priority to work with me. We met to collaborate on some new material, but it didn't pan out. The records just weren't what I was looking for, and after that, it became increasingly difficult to get ahold of him to produce new material. Eventually efforts for a second album on the label stalled, despite my solo success. It was as if my solo career was having a grand opening and a grand closing all at the same damn time.

I was torn to pieces over that, but still, I was resolute, particularly knowing that Michael was in my corner. One would think that after spending so many years in such a contentious relationship with my former manager, I'd be facing off with a bit of post-traumatic stress disorder behind this kind of business dealing. But I knew that we were on the right side of history this time. Out of his own pocket, Michael hired a team of people—publicists and a digital and social media manager—to solidify my presence and supplement everything that the label was supposed to be doing for me as an artist while we tried to hash out how to move on to a second record.

While I was in limbo with my label, Snoop came to the rescue and took me with him to promote his album *Ego Trippin'*, on which I was featured. One of the songs I sang on was "Can't Say Goodbye," which we performed on "Idol Gives Back," a move that helped keep me relevant and on the scene while I figured out my next moves. I am grateful to Snoop for that opportunity, but also, again, for the friendship and good times he provided during that unsure period. When Snoop and I got together, it was never just business as usual; he understood how to be productive and have fun, which was exactly what I needed. A funny story: One night while Snoop and I were out promoting *Ego Trippin'*, his manager invited us to dinner to celebrate her birthday, promising that in addition to a fine meal, she would introduce us to Michael Strahan, the pro football player who'd just won the Super Bowl with his team, the New York Giants. I was a huge fan of Strahan's, so naturally, I was excited and anxious to meet him. By the time dinner ended, though, he still hadn't made it to the restaurant. We waited as long as we could, but with a full lineup of promotional events set up for the next morning, disappointed, Michael Paran finally decided we needed to leave and called our driver to meet us out front. Michael was having a hard time getting our driver to answer his phone, though, and he, Snoop, and I were getting increasingly frustrated waiting in the lobby for our ride. Just as Michael headed over to tell us that he couldn't get the driver on the line, a man dressed in a suit exited a black SUV and entered the restaurant. Annoyed, Michael asked him, "Where have you been?," thinking it was our driver at last. The man looked at Michael and walked past him and right up to Snoop and me: "Uncle Charlie!" he boomed.

It was Michael Strahan!

Snoop and I fell out in laughter as Michael Strahan tossed his head in Michael Paran's direction and asked, "Who is that guy over there?"

I apologized to him. "Obviously, he didn't know who you are, but I do," I said quickly. "I'm so happy to meet you. I'm a big fan."

Neither Snoop nor I have ever let my stepson live that evening down. "Dude," I say to him, "you called Michael Strahan our driver. What is wrong with you? That man won the Super Bowl." We still chuckle at that one.

When we weren't out promoting *Ego Trippin'*, my anxiety level increased. This impasse with the record label lasted four years, and frankly, it scared me. I was questioning whether I could put out a record on my own and whether it would be a hit without R. Kelly's work on it. I wasn't being paranoid, either: the label was insisting that its intention was to put out another R. Kelly–executive–produced Charlie Wilson album, and it gave not-so-subtle hints that it did not believe my work would do well without him. It was Michael and Mahin who finally said, "Go find your own records and produce them yourself." Their unwavering support, once again, was evident. I was trying to play by the rules and waiting for the record company to do what it was supposed to do, and my wife and manager saw something different—understood that I had the talent, capability, and wherewithal to capitalize on the success of *Charlie, Last Name Wilson* and keep doing what I love to do: make music and perform. It was an interesting time in my musical journey because on one hand, I was a newly minted solo artist, but on the other, I was a veteran who had been making records for more than thirty years. Michael and Mahin were right: I knew how to produce a record. I could do it.

And so I did. I got my own songwriters and producers and set about recording my own records. I soon discovered, however, that it was easier said than done to produce my own album. Try as I might, I couldn't find that feel that I was looking for— that surefire Charlie Wilson sound. And while I struggled, the record label, aware of and upset by the fact that R. Kelly was not going to be working with me on the next album, had me feeling like it was simply waiting for me to crash so that it would have a justification for dropping me. But God hadn't brought me that far for me to fail.

. . .

I had several songs that I liked for my new album, but for a long time, I felt as if something was missing. It wasn't an option for me to go back to the label with records that were just "okay." I needed a smash hit, a single that I thought would live up to the songs that made my solo career pop. It was then that my wife reminded me about a CD of songs one of my staff producers, Gregg Pagani, had given me the week before. We were in the car, and really, there was nothing else to listen to, so I popped that CD into the player. Initially, nothing really appealed to me, but then I heard the opening to "There Goes My Baby." It had a vintage feel to it, and the words were on point.

"Woooooo! Who the hell is that?" I said when that vocal went to the chorus. We were five blocks from the house but it took us two hours to get home. I kept replaying it as we drove—must have listened to it at least thirty times before we pulled into the driveway. My wife said, "Honey, I'm telling you right now: you have to do that record. If you don't do that record, something is wrong with you."

I called Gregg right away and asked if that song was free and clear. He told me a young guy by the name of Calvin Richardson had written it with Babyface, and it was, indeed, available.

"I'll be there first thing tomorrow," I told Gregg. "I want that one."

The next day, I went into the studio and put my own touch on it. If you heard Calvin's version, it would give you chills. Even my wife says, "Yeah, you sang it, but not as good as him! He tore it up!" He's incredible, as is the song. I play it at my shows and every time I sing it, the people get up on their feet. I wish I had written that one.

After I put my vocals on "There Goes My Baby," I started playing it for other people to get their feedback and everyone had the same reaction my wife and I had in the car that day: they loved it. Excited that I'd finally found the hit that was going to drive the second album of my burgeoning solo career, Michael sent the song to the label for its review. Immediately, label heads sent back their verdict: the song, they said, sounded "old" and "dated," and they wanted to meet with me to figure out how to "contemporize" the song.

When I showed up for that meeting, though, the record label executives weren't interested in talking about "There Goes My Baby" or even my new album. Instead, the head of the label called me into his office and said, "I want to play something for you." The record on his stereo: Billy Ocean's "Suddenly."

For the life of me, I couldn't figure out why this man was playing this record for me. I listened politely, waiting for him to get to the point. When it ended, what he offered blew me away: "Charlie," he said, "this is the song you need to do. This is the kind of song people are waiting for from you. Could you do this cover for me?"

I was frozen, unable to push any words out of my mouth. I wanted to tell him to go kick rocks. But my kinder, gentler side prevailed: "What will you do with the record if I record it?" I asked.

"We will put it out and it will go to all the soccer moms. They will love it!" he said insistently.

There was much more said during that meeting, but the bottom line was that I had a hit record in my hands and all the record label wanted to do was have me sing a cover for my next big single. My spirit was crushed.

Later, I made it clear that I was committed to releasing what I wanted, rather than what they thought would be best. The executives warned me: "If you put that record out, it will be the end of your career." They also made their stance on "There Goes My Baby" and me very clear to Michael, going so far as to tell him that they would have "never signed Charlie Wilson with this record."

Still, I refused. If I was going to go down in flames, I wanted it to be on my own terms, with a song I believed in. Michael told the label this, and so, angry as the executives were, they capitulated. After a four-year wait for another R. Kelly song, an epic battle with the label, and a commitment to do the kind of music I loved and that I knew my fans would appreciate, I handed over "There Goes My Baby" and announced that I wanted it to be my next single. Still, the executives overseeing my projects tried to sabotage it in every way. There was no artwork for the CD they sent to the radio stations; instead, someone's secretary wrote, "There Goes My Baby," with a Sharpie on the plain white cover and mailed it out like it was a demo. A piece of trash.

When we did put it out, that record instantly took off. The jocks started playing it everywhere. It debuted at number two with a bullet on the *Billboard* Hot R&B/Hip-Hop Songs chart and sat at number one for ten weeks, which was sign enough of its success. But the real nod came the night I sang it for the first time in a show, at the Hard Rock Hotel and Casino in Biloxi, Mississippi. When I got to the chorus, my vocals were practically drowned out by the crowd as every person from the front row to the bar way in the back sang the words at the top of their lungs. I was stunned, as was my team, which was standing in the crowd, by the sound board. "That song is going to change your career," Michael said insistently. He was right. I had another hit.

Despite the song's success, though, the label would not pay for a video for "There Goes My Baby." Undeterred, Michael and I decided to make one on our own, and we agreed to make it personal. Right around that time, Snoop surprised Shante with a vow-renewal ceremony at my ranch. As I wrote earlier, as a gift, I performed and dedicated "There Goes My Baby" to them during their first dance. What better way to illustrate the song than with footage compiled from their epic ceremony?

We got their permission to use clips from the ceremony and Michael convinced the director of Snoop's reality TV show, a recovering addict who had been inspired by my own addiction story, to allow us to use clips from *Snoop Dogg's Father Hood* to make the video. Though we paid for the video out of our own pockets, we did have one minor blip in its release: the E! network, which owned the rights to Snoop's show, initially refused to license the footage. But Michael was able to convince them to let us use it, and the video eventually got made and distributed. It was so touching, particularly the scene at the end when Snoop gets teary-eyed, revealing his vulnerability as a husband and father. It was a testament to the fact that every setback we faced was followed with a much bigger blessing, the kind that gave me the strength to push through the doubt. I knew deep down in my heart that God had bigger plans for me and if I just kept moving forward, I would succeed.

And I did. "There Goes My Baby" received a Grammy Award nomination for Best Male R & B Vocal Performance in

2009, and made it onto both the *Billboard* Hot 100 and th
Billboard US R & B/Hip-Hop charts before being named *Bil*
board's number one Urban Adult song for 2009. Its album
Uncle Charlie, also enjoyed an incredible run on the charts, de-
buting at number two on the Billboard Top 200 and number
two on the Top R&B chart, earning its own Grammy nod for
Best R & B Album.

That year after the big Grammy ceremony, while attend-
ing the Sony Music after-party with my fellow label mates and
friends Usher and John Legend, as luck would have it, I ran into
the head of the label. There we were, standing face-to-face, and
all I could think about was that moment when I was in his office
and he broke my spirit. A whirlwind of emotions washed over
me. I don't know if it was the look in my eyes that compelled
him to say it, but, after a moment, the executive said, "I have to
tell you, Charlie, I was wrong."

I was shocked. "I'm going to need to hear you say that one
more time," I said.

He dropped his head. "I'm telling you right now, I was
wrong," he said.

"Thank you," I said, smiling.

I have to give the man credit: he had the decency to apologize to me, something most other business executives would
never do. I appreciated that, and to this day, I respect him for
that.

Then, as if to put the exclamation point on an incredible evening, as I was leaving the party, I ran into Beyoncé and Jay Z, just
as they were exiting their SUV. As soon as Beyoncé saw me, she
started singing a verse from "Charlie, Last Name Wilson" with

that beautiful voice of hers, through that beautiful smile. Jay Z topped that with a boisterous, "Uncle Charlie!" What an incredible night!

It was official: Charlie Wilson was no longer just the voice behind The GAP Band. I was a bona fide solo artist.

With that decision came a lot of change. Michael hired a new band, consisting primarily of church folk who were respectful and, most important, listened to and took direction. And he got a bit of "act right" out of the promoters, who were finally getting word about how professional and direct my team was and how incredible and receptive audiences were to my new solo show. Mahin chipped in to help organize the show and pick out a new wardrobe for my stage performances, and we hired a dynamic social media expert, Jenna Lankford, to put together a viable online campaign that built up my following and rewarded my fans with videos and pictures of me and my show. I was at a whole new level when I went out on my own—and people in the industry recognized it. Indeed, several artists actually approached Michael to ask him to manage their careers, too, but he refused; he was too focused on taking me to heights I'd never before seen. For instance, I had been trying for years to get onto the lineup as a solo artist on the Essence Music Festival tour, a hugely popular multiday concert series in New Orleans created and sponsored by *Essence* magazine, but they wouldn't have me until I officially went solo and Michael went to bat for me. I'd already performed the festival with The GAP Band in 2003, but it took three years for me to get invited back as a solo artist to the 2006 EMF festival, which was held that year in Houston after Hurricane Katrina made it

impossible to set up in New Orleans. The festival's organizers said they were impressed with my solo performance, but when I asked to return the next year, they told me that they rarely did repeat performances. Three more years passed before they invited me back again, this time to the 2009 festival, buoyed by the success of "There Goes My Baby." Sure enough, after that performance, I became one of the rare artists to get invited back every year since then, making me what many consider a staple of the Essence Music Festival. I'm happy to perform for the festival's enthusiastic fans, music lovers all.

I've since been invited to countless music festivals, exposing me to an even bigger audience. A highlight has been performing overseas for the troops in Iraq and Kuwait, an experience I enjoyed so much that I went back five consecutive years. The first time I performed for the troops, in 2009, it was during the time *Uncle Charlie* was being released. Most celebrities wouldn't dare miss a promotional week to support their new album, but I felt strongly about accepting the opportunity to support our troops. The day my album came out, Michael went on the Internet to see how it had debuted on the charts and shared the great news with me over lunch. I was so happy I almost broke down into tears right there in the dining facility, in front of all the soldiers with whom we were lunching.

But my presence there wasn't about me. It was about the troops. With a few of my band members and dancers in tow, I stood in front of an audience of men and women who put their lives on the line for our country and, through my art, from my heart, gave them the morale boost they needed to soldier on. I'll never forget strapping into that Black Hawk, wrapped in a bulletproof vest that felt like it weighed sixty pounds, hanging on for dear life as we zipped over Baghdad, the sweltering, sprawling earth spread out beneath us. When we landed on the base, we were hustled to our accommodations, no different from those occupied by the soldiers—tents that sleep ten to twenty people. The air rang with the sound of gunfire and helicopters, the hum of war. Sleep proved elusive; I was scared. We all were. But God was with us. "We have the best security team there is in the whole world with us: the US military," I kept saying, to relax my team and, also, myself.

All that fear shook itself loose, though, when I climbed up on that stage in front of the troops and sang my songs. The dust storms were brutal on my throat, as was the blistering heat. But we fought through it all and tore up that stage anyway, and those men and women sang and danced right along with me and later happily met with me for autographs and pictures. It was an amazing time, despite what I consider to be a brush with near-death in Iraq. It was early in the morning; we were preparing to fly to another city in Iraq to perform when my wife made it clear that we should get going, stat.

"I don't feel comfortable staying here," she kept saying. "We should leave right away."

And so we did. Not ten minutes after we got to the airport, one of the majors brought the grim news: "A missile landed at the base you just left," he said.

Though a rocket had hit the side of the building in which we'd been working, by the grace of God, no one was hurt. But who knows if that would have been the case if we'd stayed any longer than we did.

All of this is to say that as a solo artist, I entered an entirely different realm of performance, of possibility. My wife once said to me, "God will do everything for you on his time, not on your time." No truer words could have been said. For example, Michael hired an agent for me, Mark Siegel, and many more amazing opportunities opened up for me. Like in 2009, I was asked by legendary basketball player Michael Jordan to perform for his celebrity guests during his popular golf tournament in the Bahamas. I was thankful for the opportunity, but more, I recognized the importance of it: there were many high-profile people in the audience, and I knew that I needed to leave it all on the stage so that every person who could hear my voice would remember my performance. Derek Jeter was so moved by it that, after my show, he invited me to join him during his poker game. I don't gamble, so there was no use for me at the table, but I did go over to him. Derek told me I'd given one of the best performances he'd ever seen. I was humbled by that. A couple years later, he asked me to perform at one of his charity events, and I gladly obliged.

In The GAP Band, there were three people who each wanted to be in control but didn't want to take responsibility beyond the making of the music, and a manager who seemed to me to want to break us emotionally, mentally, and physically. But out on my own, with a wife who loves and protects me, a manager who is excellent at what he does and whom I can trust, and a new lease on life—stronger, sober, and wiser musically than I've ever been—everything just feels right. It is right because this time around, I'm doing it my way and I'm on a path informed by so much that I've learned along the way.

I go back to the same places where I performed when I was high—the same places where, earlier in my career, addicted and broke, I could have died, places that remind me of some of the things I did in those dark corners filled with shadows and painful memories. Initially, when I found myself in familiar venues, I would stay in the hotel room, go do the show, go back to the hotel room, and go to sleep and try to block out all memories of that city and what I did there. In the beginning, it was heart wrenching and terrifying. I stayed in prayer over it. And I kept a support system around me so that I wouldn't sink back into the behavior from my days with The GAP Band.

Beyond that, as a solo artist who is sober, I've learned to be really clear about my needs. Back in the day, I loaded up my contract rider with all kinds of demands for alcohol. In the beginning I demanded gin gimlets, and then Long Island iced teas were my drink of choice. I needed to have them before I got onstage because that would warm me up and, I thought, get me ready for the crowd. Of course, that would trigger my other addictions, and much later, when The GAP Band was going into the toilet, I'd smoke or hit the pipe before going onto the stage. But as a sober solo artist, I realized that I didn't need anything to sing. And I don't need anyone around me who does. In fact, smoking, drinking, doing drugs, and frequenting bars isn't allowed while touring with my show. If I catch anybody at the bar before we have a show, they're fired on the spot. It's in the contract, and everybody has to sign it—background dancers, singers, road managers, managers, musicians, security, and anyone else necessary for the show to go on. I have a zero-tolerance policy for drugs and alcohol. Don't even let me think you're doing anything, much less smell it on you. If you even *think* about it in my presence, it's grounds for termination. Because on my tour, in my set, we are all natural.

This is rare in my business, but it is my way.

When you're young and strong, it's easy to get onstage and use every part of your being to do your best. Some people turn to drugs and alcohol to boost their talents, for that lift they need to be energized and excited and to keep up the show. After a while, you rely on those things to hit your notes. Getting sober will really bring you back to reality and have you questioning whether you can do your job. I give 100 percent to anything I do, but I have to dig deeper to get some particularly challenging notes out. Indeed, more effort than ever before is required because I'm older. My little brother used to always say, "Charlie Wilson, change the keys to the songs to make it easier." I tried that so it would make singing certain songs feel more comfortable, but it didn't sit right with me. Ultimately, I refused to change the keys to all the songs I did in the eighties. I realized I just had to push harder to get them right. A lot of people don't want to work that hard to hit those notes. They use alternate notes or sing around the original songs, or try to figure out how to change up the notes they can't handle. I choose to go after the sound that's on the record—the sound I felt when I first wrote the songs and the melody that poured out of my heart. I do this because that's what makes people sing along with me. People want to hear the records that bring back memories. I put tremendous effort into making that happen for folks. It drives me crazy to hear people altering the notes and doing a jazz version or a hip-hop version of their song. I don't want to hear a reggae version of a record that I fell in love with years ago.

When I hear that band start, I hit that stage in rare form. I'm not taking people on a slow ride they really don't want to be on. I'm sending people back down memory lane and giving them new courage.

Besides my energy coming from my new attitude and my renewed faith, the money is also different. Today, I make more money in one show than I did in my entire time with The GAP Band. When I consider all that I lost—the opportunity to support my family, to plan for my retirement, and even to enjoy some of the material things I never had a chance to purchase for myself—I get a little angry about it. My wife tells me to let it go, to be grateful that things are different today. As ever, she is right. And so it is. I am so grateful.

. . .

The GAP Band is never far away from my heart. After our lawsuit against Lonnie, my brother Ronnie eventually decided to leave show business altogether and vowed never to set foot back on the stage again. Today, he sings for God. My brother Robert, who passed from a heart attack, is *with* God. We'd been talking about his joining me on tour and had planned to meet up in New York City to discuss details when, the day before I was to see him, I got the tragic news that my little brother had died. My heart is broken over that.

At the beginning of my solo career, when I was onstage, I would look over my shoulder and reminisce, however briefly, about performing with my brothers in front of throngs of people. I missed them. I missed us. But being a solo star was the right choice. Finally, I am in charge, making my own decisions, living my life and my passion out loud, sans the drama.

This is the new beginning my father saw in his vision.

Chapter 13

The Art of Song

Whether I am performing as a solo artist or as a member of a band, I'm only as good as the songs I sing. A great song is so much more than a snappy hook and a few well-placed "please baby" appeals purred by a good-looking, scantily clad bombshell. Unforgettable music, the kind that informs the soundtrack of your childhood, that you snapped your fingers to at the family reunion, that you made a point of playing at your wedding, that was there when you made babies of your own or will be there when you plan to, is persuasive. It is seductive and authentic. A *feeling*. Those melodies, arrangements, and lyrics dig deep into the emotional well of the listener.

As a songwriter, it is my responsibility—indeed, my joy—to find a level of reality for the listeners; I am charged with reminding them of that love, of that desire, of that newness, of that loss and heartache, that longing when the one they want gets away, and, too, of the satisfaction they feel when life is fulfilling. The music that lifts the words, and the emotion I bring to it with my singing, is the ultimate form of communication for me; it lets me connect physically, spiritually, and emotionally with others, surely in a way that extends far beyond any face-to-face talk I could sit and have with another human being. It is a conversation with the soul.

I know for sure that I gathered up the tools I needed to form my own style of musical expression from my mother, while watching her practice songs she would later play for Sunday service. Sitting at her knee while she worked through the melodies was a master class on how to inject soul into a song. She would smooth out that sheet music and sit it up there on that piano ledge and study it, boldly deconstructing the block and Gothic chords meant for Catholic church pipe organs into expressive feasts, which she would serve up on the piano and the Hammond B3 organ. Under my mother's fingers, those regular notes on the one, three, and five would find themselves on the seventh, ninth, and raised nine—a change that instantly colored the sound in deep, smoky hues full of that deep-down-to-the-gut soul. By the time she finished flipping it, that Catholic church music would almost sound like funk. I tried to watch her hands—her fingers moved so fast—but rarely could I keep up. That didn't stop me from trying, though. My go-to chord was B-flat, and I'd mimic what she was doing in my own way. She'd listen and smile that easy smile and encourage me to keep going. "Baby, everybody can't sing in B-flat," she would say. But come Sunday, when she was on the piano and I was sitting on that bench in front of the organ, playing alongside her, she would go to B-flat anyway, so I could play. That black key—the B-flat and the A-flat—I could slide all around those, and she would let me fly.

My fascination with chord structures and the infusion of soul into my presentation of music certainly played itself out on the stages of the local clubs in Tulsa when my boys and I were performing all those Top 40 hits recorded by white artists but enjoyed by our mostly black audience.

To understand what I mean, consider the difference between the way Leon Russell sang his piece "A Song for You" and the way Donny Hathaway, a genius composer and songwriter in his own right, came back and flipped it with his own special brew. I'd heard and played Leon's version plenty of times while The GAP Band toured with him back in the early seventies; he would play the piano part and sing it with this twang—a bluesy, folkish offering that was, indeed, beautiful. But boy, when I heard Donny's version! He made all that soul grate the notes while his butter-soft delivery took listeners straight to church—that kind of down-home, early-Sunday-morning sound that would make you hop out of your church pew and spread your arms wide in exaltation, maybe even coax a few extra dollars out of your pocket for the collection plate. Though I dug Leon's version, Donny's made me feel some kind of way—made me want to sing it with all my might.

All that is to say that as much musicality as I had in me fresh out of high school, as good as I was at slathering Top 40 hits with all kinds of soul, I still didn't know a real song when I heard it—hadn't quite figured out yet how to flip a beautiful melody in the way that Donny did with "A Song for You." Sure, I could add my own flavor to a song, but flipping the melody was something that was a work in progress for me. (By the way, to this day, I feel like Leon's catalog is a gold mine for some really big songs that would fly with a little soul sprinkled on the melodies. I always loved his "Lady Blue" and "Tight Rope," and though he went through a serious brain operation in the not-too-distant past, he's simply too talented and deeply rooted in beautiful music to be counted out.)

I did try to formalize my sound as a student at Langston University, where I studied music for a short stint, but I couldn't find my musical legs there. There was one professor, Professor B, who simply didn't understand what I was trying to do—who didn't respect it—and that played a huge role in my decision to quit seeking that inspiration in a formal setting. One day while still at the university, I was in one of those practice rooms playing all kinds of music I'd picked up, including that of Donald Byrd and Quincy Jones. I was trying to decipher the chord structures when one of the professors walked in and announced that I was playing too loudly. "Would you quiet it down, son?" he asked.

I closed the door and didn't think much more about it. Twenty minutes later, there he was at the door again.

"What do you want, man?" I asked, this time annoyed.

"Mr. Wilson, those chord structures don't exist and I wish you wouldn't play those kinds of chords here in the music hall."

"They don't exist?" I spat, incredulous. "So you're telling me Quincy Jones doesn't know what he's doing? I'm playing what I heard."

I acknowledge that when it came to musical theory, I was a little slower than my other friends. I was fast at putting notes on the page and had an innate feeling for how a song should go, but all the other things that went into writing and composing were less intuitive. Plus, Professor B, a white man, just seemed to have it out for me, which I experienced time and again. I remember one day going into the auditorium to listen to this great organist Jimmy McGriff. Later, I'd try to play his solos exactly the way I heard them and analyze the chord structure, what made them special, after which I would walk into Professor B's class, where, arms folded, he would be waiting to lay into me. The theory they taught at Langston was not black; it was distinctively white. For a student interested in playing chords that had an R & B and jazz feel to them, it was a poor fit. Professor B would make a point of making me feel like the style of music I was drawn to was dishonest, wrong, somehow. I would put the grit into the chords and he would say, "Well, what do you want, Mr. Wilson? A knife to the face?"

"Yeah! Sounds good to me!" I'd say right back.

Professor B and I were too far apart to bridge the gap. We were like oil and water. Plus, I figured out pretty quickly that I didn't need the theory, really; I could hear something and could tell someone else to play it if I needed to. Everything I've done to date—every horn part, every bass part, every hit record— has come to fruition with me humming the notes to people and saying, "Play this guitar part here, play this drum part here." My ears are very good. Eventually I left Langston after two years and learned my craft through listening and collaborating with the best.

I had already gotten my BA at Irma Wilson's knee and my doctorate in the streets. Yet some of my earliest and most valuable lessons on the art of collaboration came while working with Leon. The sound we created together was otherworldly—

a melding of folk and funk, rock and blues, with a pinch of Baptist gospel and some bluegrass vocal squalling lifting it up to the heavens. Fusing it all together made it incredible—pure madness. While working with him, The GAP Band met some of the most influential people in the world at that time: George Harrison, Ringo Starr, Billy Preston, Jimmy Cliff, Bob Marley, Bob Dylan, Eric Clapton. Everybody would come through Leon's studio—so many incredible guitarists, singers, and keyboardists, all gathered in the name of stellar music. Stevie Wonder came through one time and I was watching him like a hawk—staring a hot hole into his head. I couldn't take my eyes off his movements, and I mimicked each and every one, reveling in his musical moments. We also found ourselves, one day, in a studio jam session with Ringo Starr on the drums and George Harrison standing in the corner. It took all I had not to yell out, "There are two Beatles in this room!" There I was playing little clubs with no more than one hundred and fifty people one minute, and the next, I was in a room with the royalty of music—people who sold out stadiums. My nerves definitely got in my way, but I learned quickly to do whatever they were doing as if I was a part of the room—as if I was supposed to be there. Every once in a while I would throw my voice out there: "I think we should add just a little guitar right there," I'd say, or, "Can we add a little percussion right there? What do you think of that, Leon?"

"That's a good idea," Leon would say easily.

In time, I started talking in the room, actually believing I was supposed to be there. George Harrison and all those guys would be looking and I'd start saying crazy stuff because much of what they were saying didn't make sense sometimes, either. Young and eager, I'd say, "Yeah, yeah—that's right!" and then add something completely off the wall and they'd think it was cool. But that's collaboration—being in a room where passion is thick and everyone is dedicated to putting forth ideas that, in the end, will make something beautiful. Something unforgettable.

The thrill of creation is indescribable. Magical. And my brothers and I took great pleasure and pride in our art. It was as if we were a bunch of chefs, mixing this with that, tossing beats and guitar licks and runs on the keyboards and blasts of the horns into a stew of funk and soul to feed to the people. That's what we called it; "cooking in the kitchen." We were taking all these different sounds bouncing around inside our heads and mixing them up and cooking them down. We would do all kinds of out-of-the-box, creative things, such as run my voice through the E-mu synthesizer to see how it would distort the sound, or tape ourselves singing, then run the tape backward in playback to see what kind of noise it would produce. The music would whiz and whir, with the beat sliding right on the front of the song from the back side. In fact, a small bass line in "Oops Up Side Your Head" is the bass played backward. We discovered it while we were running the tape onto another reel and we pulled the head back to hear the music in the direction it was going. At first it wasn't making any sound, but when we slowed down the speed so that we could hear the music playing, we liked what we heard and put a beat to it. You can't really hear it; it's buried in there. So is my trademark giggle. That made it onto "Oops" during one particular recording session when

I burst out laughing at someone in the control room while the microphone was on. The engineers erased most of it, but my brother liked how one part sounded and said, "Let's keep that." It became such an iconic sound on that record that we decided to use it again in our work, along with my signature scats, "shabadodadweedopdeedop" and "oooohweeee." Those made their way into my musical lexicon while I was trying to find the melody on the GAP Band song "I'm in Love." I didn't have any words yet, so I just improvised the phrasing with an assortment of sounds that came to me as I worked out the piece in the studio—sounds that I had no intention, really, of keeping once I found the right lyrics. But one night while we were finishing up the song, a woman who was there listening to us tinker with the final pieces almost lost her mind when we started to erase those ad-libs. "You're going to mess with that?" she exclaimed. "Don't mess with that; it's the best part!"

"What is?" I asked, confused.

"All that shabadodah stuff," she said. "I love that part."

Those scats didn't make it into the final version of the song, but I ended up using them on many others, so much so that I became the "shabadodadweedopdeedop" and "oooohweeee" man. I didn't fully embrace it initially, but my fans love it, so here I am, all these years later, still incorporating them into my songs and stage performances.

Each of these things adds to the dynamic of the songs, much like any ingredient does to an outstanding dish. You may not be able to call out all the components of that meal, but it sure wouldn't taste the same if you skimped on an element or two.

On the subject of musical creativity, I must reference one pioneer in particular. Sitting down at a piano with Stevie Wonder is, by far, the most incredible experience I've ever had making music. When you're with him and he's creating, it's as if you've turned on a tap and it's overflowing with music. You have no idea if what he is doing is something coming off the top of his head or if he's playing something he's long had and never shared with anyone. Regardless, the flow and the energy that he elicits is magic. "Musical genius" doesn't even begin to describe Stevie's ability to convey emotion through lyrics, notes, melody, and harmony. There's no way to describe it other than to say it is God-given.

I first met him in the early seventies; The GAP Band was working on *Magicians Holiday*, and I was picked to go to the studio and mix it, at a place called the Record Plant. Stevie was in there, running late. In other words, he was rolling into my time. The engineer, who had already heard our songs, told Stevie about "this guy named Charles Wilson." Stevie asked to see me and I started shaking like a leaf. When they played my record a little bit, he began rolling his head as he usually does, and he beckoned me to the piano. I sat while he played, thinking my teeth would shatter from the nervous energy I put forth meeting my childhood idol. And then he gave me a note to sing and I sang it. We went from there, me sitting with the legend, singing, playing, and creating. You couldn't tell me anything after that. He hugged me before I left, and I thought, "Man, some of that rubbed off on me. I know I'm about to make it big!"

That was the beginning of a friendship. He's an incredible person—one I love to death. I asked him years ago if he would write a song for me and he would always tell me, "Quit begging!" He said, "I'm going to play on a GAP Band record!" It took him about six years to get there, but he got there. We had a song called "Someday We'll All Be Free," and Coretta Scott King wanted it as a theme song to try to get her husband's birthday made into a national holiday. My manager wanted to make a lot of money off of the song, but I don't think he understood the true meaning behind it. It wasn't about the money. It was about the legacy. So we never got to have it used in that way. But the musical relationship between Stevie and myself is forever sealed. As is our friendship.

Of course, memories of my brothers and I creating together stretch far and long and wide, and it makes me proud to know that the power and legacy of what we cooked up all those years ago manifests itself in places where the heart reveals itself—on the dance floor at weddings, out in the park at family reunions, on road-trip playlists, and in the most intimate spaces, too, of lovers meeting lip to lip, body to body, heart to heart. The feeling that comes from knowing I've had a hand in people's lives is overwhelming—almost as good as the feeling I get when I'm onstage. That's my favorite moment of all—looking out over the audience, immersed in the moment as the energy that went into creating the hits transfers from my heart to the people who've long loved my songs. It's as if the seeds I planted all those years ago—the bass lines, the melodies, the lyrics, the vocals—are all blooming right before my eyes, over and over again. When I get to the chorus and everybody is swaying and singing the words with me, that's exquisite.

I must admit that I never really understand artists who

say they're tired of singing their hits and, in some cases, vow never to sing them. Those songs are hits for a very specific reason—not just because we had the wherewithal to make something great, but because the fans loved them and lifted them up. I never tire of singing "Outstanding," because the people just keep losing their minds every time they hear it. Every generation that's heard it since it debuted in 1982 has had the same reaction. "Outstanding" is timeless.

The way the song came about is kind of sweet. Our drummer, Raymond Calhoun, came to the studio with this beat and a little bit of the bass line and melody. He was afraid to give it to me because nobody ever gave me a song that already had a melody to it. They knew that if they had a track with lyrics, they'd better just hand me the words, because as the lead singer of the group, I wanted sole say over the melody. This time Calhoun had some hints of a melody. I didn't get on him about that; I liked the spacing of the drum. Because he's a drummer, it made sense. When I first heard it, it sounded like the melody for "Three Blind Mice" in one particular key, so I took a keyboard and just started messing around with it. Soon enough, we started cooking it.

The song wasn't about any particular woman; we just got caught up in the moment with those lyrics and we were building our own beautiful woman so we could sing to her, as if she were the finest woman in the world. We asked ourselves, "What are we going to say to her?" I was never sure enough to say that to any one girl in real life; I wasn't that kind of guy. But I knew that if I put it in a song, I sure could sing it. Calhoun didn't like the idea of my changing the song around; he called the next day and said, "Uh, the bridge is in the wrong place," to which I retorted, "Calhoun, you can come back down here, but you're not touching this song. When you hear it you're going to flip out." Then I put the beat on top of it, left his keys there, and added some bass, and it turned into that iconic track. When I pulled up those vocals and my brother laid different sounds on top of my voice to layer it all out, it turned into an enduring record. When Calhoun heard it I asked, "You think it needs to be changed now?"

"No," he said, conceding. "This is great just the way it is."

Apparently, we're not the only musicians who feel this way; "Outstanding" is one of the most sampled songs in recent history. You're welcome, Mary J. Blige, Beyoncé, R. Kelly, Toni Braxton, Ice Cube, and Kid Rock, just to name a handful.

We created that same powerful musical moment when we wrote and recorded "Yearning for Your Love," another one of The GAP Band's fan favorites. That was my brother Ronnie's song. As I recall, we had just finished a show and were parked in front of the studio when my brother said, "I got something I want to play for you. There's only one thing: there's something wrong with it."

He explained that it already had a melody, which, again, everyone with whom I collaborated knew I hated. I smacked my lips in disapproval. But he kept on. "I think you're going to like this, and if you don't, you can change it and go back to the way you always do it. But give it a listen."

The track was kind of cool; Ronnie and our backup keyboardist, Oliver Scott, wrote it. When they played it, it hit me like a ton of bricks from the first note. It didn't have the guitars on it, that beginning lick. Just the piano part. But the structure of the chords was so pretty. My brother and Oliver started singing as I listened to the bridge. Suddenly, I stopped them. "Okay," I snapped. "Turn it off."

They were looking at me, their eyes searching mine. "What? You don't like it?" Ronnie asked, disappointed.

I opened the door and walked out and then I leaned back in and said, "Let's go and record it!"

We were all excited. I went in and sang it my way. I kept most of the melody the same, but I added my own flavor to it. Then my brother put his bass on the bottom of it. He tuned the strings down and it sounded like a five- or seven-string bass. Robert innovated that technique, making the sound round and big at the bottom.

We finished that record in maybe two hours, including laying down the initial instrumentation. Then we spent another three hours layering more sound on top of that and then editing it all down before we sang on top of it. We'd just come off the road, so our voices were tired, and we grew hoarse trying to get those falsetto parts to the lyric "Keep running!" But we made it beautiful. We always tracked live, meaning the four of us would play the song together during the recording, rather than recording each instrumental separately and mixing them all together. If it was good, we would catch a vibe and build from that.

I knew that song was going to be something to be dealt with later on in life, because every eight bars, I could feel myself getting chills. We called the guitar player at two a.m. and he added that lick, and we put the intro of life on it. We were lying on the floor laughing and crying and knowing that it was going to be one of the best ballads we ever had anything to do with. I'm told consistently that "Yearning for Your Love" is responsible for a generation of children. I hear it all the time: "My first child is because of you, Charlie Wilson! You and 'Yearning for Your Love.'"

Fans tend to feel the same way about "Computer Love," the hit single I helped doctor for the funk group Zapp, with Roger Troutman on his "talk box" and Shirley Murdock sharing lead vocals. I'm pleased that many of my contemporary songs are regarded in the same way. "You Are" is certainly one of those songs. That one was created in the wake of the success of "There Goes My Baby"; intent on making a song that could properly express to my wife how much she means to me, my producer and I hired an orchestra to record the strings and horns of that incredible song, and then, recognizing its magic, we released it as a single from my 2010 *Just Charlie* album. That song was number one on the Urban Adult Contemporary chart for thirteen weeks and was nominated for two Grammys, which made it a hit, but it seems to have staying power. A few times when I've sung it at concerts, men have fallen to their knees and proposed to their girlfriends, and people tell me all the time in person and via social media that they've made "You Are" the centerpiece of their wedding music, either as the song to walk down the aisle to or as the music they played for their first dance as husband and wife. It's solidified itself in the lexicon of soul music that strikes deep.

. . .

Monster hits like "Burn Rubber on Me" and "Humpin' " opened the door for hip-hop in general and New Jack Swing in particular, genres that more comfortably fit with our artistic sensibility than disco did. Total Experience tried to embrace disco but that was a fiasco, as any trip to a used-record store will demonstrate. The sounds of New Jack Swing and hip-hop were made possible by the collaborative foundations we helped to lay in the seventies and eighties, with good music that stands the test of time. Some days, I think classics such as "Outstanding," "Yearning for Your Love," and the like will be hard to come by going forward, considering how little respect is paid to true talent and, in particular, musicianship. We're living in a time, after all, where schools don't even have music programs, much less any kind of real access to instruments and all the other tools needed to foster a true love of the art form. Of course, there are exceptions. I think producers and musicians like Amir "Questlove" Thompson from the Roots, will.i.am from the Black Eyed Peas, Justin Timberlake, Beyoncé, and Pharrell Williams and the like are leading the way for this generation, pioneering new sounds and lending an aesthetic to modern music that pushes it into new and exciting directions. Consider Pharrell: He grew up immersed in the music of Charlie Wilson and The GAP Band, Marvin Gaye, and Curtis Mayfield. He knows and loves a myriad of genres of music and is genuinely inspired by that work as he creates his own hits. He's one of those connoisseurs who can tell you who played the break beat in a song from the fifties, who was on the horns on a song from the seventies, and where to find two copies of a rare record that someone wants to mine for a very specific loop. I'm beyond proud to have the music of The GAP Band be a part of what inspires artists like him.

It is that reverence that put me in the recording studio with Snoop and Master P and, eventually, chart-topping artist/producer Kanye West, with whom I have collaborated on many songs, including five on the rapper's hugely popular album *My Beautiful Dark Twisted Fantasy* and "Bound 2," a monster hit off *Yeezus*, the album he dropped in 2013. Kanye West is such a huge talent. I first met him while working on a song with Justin Timberlake and will.i.am, called "Floatin'," off the *Charlie, Last Name Wilson* project. Kanye wasn't well-known outside music industry circles, but it was clear from the start that he was gifted. That first night we met, he let us listen to "Gold Digger," the single he was preparing for release. It was clear he was about to be a big deal.

Years later, a producer suggested we meet; I drove into Los Angeles, arriving a half hour early for a session scheduled to begin at noon in order to give myself time to settle in, warm up, and then get to work. Old-school. When I arrived, I walked into the control room and asked the engineer where Kanye was. Within seconds, I felt a tap on my shoulder. It was Kanye. He was already there and ready to work.

There was no entourage, no two-hour delay, no half-assed effort. When you're in a studio with Kanye, everyone has to come dressed to impress—down to the engineers and the guys who run to get food for the crew. Even the cars he sends for the people with whom he collaborates are top-of-the-line. In Paris for a session in which we collaborated, he sent a Bentley. He is not just punctual or a perfectionist; he is a businessman. He's very knowledgeable about music and the feel of it; he knows instinctively what he wants and the kinds of sounds he's looking for and he won't stop until he finds exactly that. I know a lot of rappers, and some of them just embrace what you bring to them. Kanye searches until he is satisfied and identifies that sound before anyone else does. So as the artist he'd hired, I had to sing those parts in a way that fit his vision.

Now, this meant one of two things: we were going to bump heads like hell, or we were going to fit like a glove. Sometimes people are so creative that they can't and don't receive the creation of others—they won't open themselves up to suggestions. I haven't found that to be the case with Kanye. When I see him flowing, I get right in there and flow with him. I ease into the conversation, and he turns around and hears me singing or humming something, and after that, he says, "Go put that down!" It's a mutual respect for collaboration and creation. I like the way he operates.

A few days after we recorded those sessions in California, Kanye flew me into New York to do more work on his album. It was the week in which I lost my little brother. Just before I'd flown in to meet Kanye, I had a long discussion with Robert about working together again; we planned for him to join my band on my solo concert tour. The day after that conversation, he died. My heart ached for Robert; his death hurt me so much. It seared.

I honored him by doing what we both loved to do: I created. Kanye arranged for me to sing for the who's who of the hip-hop and R & B elite: Beyoncé, Mos Def, Nicki Minaj. He believed in my abilities so completely that while I was touring in Atlanta, he called my manager, Michael, and requested I accompany him to Paris. I got offstage that night and headed straight for an overnight flight to France, and I stayed there working in the studio with Kanye for a week or two. Soon after that, he flew me back to Paris again to perform with him on two television shows, one in Paris, the other in London; both times we performed "Bound 2," from his album *Yeezus*. Kanye is not only a visionary, he's an all-around good guy for whom I have nothing but love.

I feel the same about Justin Timberlake, an artistic genius in his own right. I first met Justin on the set of Snoop's music video for "Signs." Before our work was done, he was proclaiming that he wanted to produce a record for my next album, and I was excited by the prospect. He ended up cowriting "Floatin'"with will.i.am, a song on my *Charlie, Last Name Wilson* album. My respect for and admiration of his talent is matched only by that which I have for Pharrell Williams, whom I've known a lifetime. I met him when he was just finding his footing in hip-hop; he asked me to sing on some tracks he'd been working on, and upon hearing his genius, I happily agreed. "You're going to be big," I told him back then, not to flatter, but because I honestly believed this to be true. His sound was otherworldly—stretched beyond the confines of what is normally acceptable for rap song production. Still, he was so shy. I remember I had a GAP Band show in New York and I invited Pharrell to watch. When I called him to the stage, he was so nervous he refused to come out, but my wife pushed him out there with me. It has been great watching him come into his own. Eventually, I got to work with him again, this time on the hugely popular Snoop Dogg hit "Beautiful."

Kanye. Justin. Pharrell. All of them are my musical nephews, and I was privileged to share the stage with two of them—Justin and Pharrell—along with Snoop, at the 2013 BET Honors awards show, where I was given a lifetime achievement award. To perform with them in front of industry hit makers and legends was a career highlight. The celebration kicked off with peers I have long respected—India.Arie, Jamie Foxx, and one of my musical idols, Stevie Wonder—standing before me on that glorious stage, singing my songs, with hundreds of people, celebrities and fans alike, rocking along with them. I was blessed to sit front and center to receive both the love and the energy emanating not just from the performances but the people who were enjoying them with me. But the true splendor of the moment came when it was my turn to take that stage with Snoop, Justin, and Pharrell. Weeks before, Michael had gushed about it all, his words giving me the armor I needed to take the stage confidently. "You're going to smash this thing like no one else has ever done," he said. But Snoop, along with Justin and Pharrell, who flew in from Europe just to join me onstage, gave me the air I needed to soar.

We had practiced that performance only twice—once the night before the show's taping, and then again on the day of, when we worked together to block out our dance steps on the fully dressed stage. Justin was genius—arranging the horn section and tossing to the band ideas on how to transition from song to song in rehearsal, then honoring me with an introduction that made my heart full. By the time we took the stage, we were each so pumped that our excitement alone would have coaxed even the most reluctant spectator out of his seat.

Our presentation was electric. We played a twenty-six-minute set (it was originally scheduled to be only six minutes, but the show's producers saw us rehearse the longer version and graciously extended our time) and my heart became all the more full with every second I was up there, shoulder to shoulder with my nephews, working up that sweat and raising this beautiful voice God saw fit to give me. Looking out over that audience, I saw everyone—from the hardest gangsta rapper to the most glamorous movie starlet—out of their seat waving their hands in the air, hitting their two-step and singing my songs at the top of their lungs. Truly, that was a gift. All I'd ever wanted, all I'd ever dreamed about, from the first time I'd taken the stage as a kid, was that dynamic—that momentum between me and the people I was charged with entertaining. When that hits, it is the ultimate collaboration.

Stevie Wonder was so sick that he couldn't even make it to rehearsals or sound check; I wasn't sure he was going to make it at all. He showed up fifteen minutes before the tribute, ready to perform. I was ecstatic that my friend and childhood idol was able to make it. He later told me that nothing could have stopped him from being there for me that day.

Of course, I wanted Kanye to be a part of my tribute, but it didn't work out. After the performance, he left his then-girlfriend Kim Kardashian and their newborn daughter to surprise me at Michael's house, where he waited to congratulate me in person. That action spoke to the kind of person he is. We talked and laughed for a while before the rerun of the awards show came on and he said, "Let's watch it together." And so we did.

Chapter 14

What Doesn't Kill You

Mahin, Michael, and I went to the Bahamas several years ago and my engineer Michael Evans, a boat enthusiast, had brought us out on the ocean to enjoy the beauty that God made when he and my wife convinced me that I should get into the water. I was frightened to death of the ocean because of, well, sharks. Maybe I saw *Jaws* one too many times, but it was enough to convince me that I didn't want to be anybody's bait. Still, the water was clear, the sun was high, the air was warm, we were anchored just off the shore of a beautiful island, and between making fun of and laughing at me, Mahin and Michael convinced me that really, the chances of my being eaten alive by a shark were minuscule enough to take a chance and get on in. Besides, Michael was telling me fantastic tales of diving down into the water and looking at the wonders of the deep blue, and, really, I wanted to see it for myself.

I'm a strong swimmer and don't normally wear fins. But for some reason, I decided to slide them onto my feet and jump into the crystal-clear water. And boy, was it incredible. I saw coral heads, reefs galore, and yellowtail—dozens of them in a school, swimming close enough for me to reach out and touch them all. And then, quick as a wink, all those fish just took off, as if fleeing from something. The first thing I thought was, "Shark!" I panicked like you wouldn't believe—taking in air and splashing all around and trying my best to get back up the ladder of the boat with those giant fins on. The more I struggled, the more I kept slipping off the ladder and flailing all about, out of breath and absolutely sure I was about to be devoured alive.

Finally, after several minutes of thrashing and falling and clinging to the ladder for dear life, I made it up the steps and spilled myself onto the deck of the boat, exhausted, out of breath, heart racing, believing for sure that I'd narrowly escaped death and certain that a shark did, indeed, bite off both my legs, because I'd heard somewhere that if a shark attacks you, your body goes into such shock that it doesn't know limbs have been ripped from you. And then I looked over at my wife on the other side of the boat, feeding the fish. Here I was, sure I was about to die, struggling to get on this boat, and nobody was paying me any kind of mind! When they finally did notice me, Mahin broke the silence: "What's wrong with you? We're feeding fish!" With my heart about to pop out of my chest and my hands frantically checking for my limbs, I told them all about my trauma, and they just laughed and laughed at me and my shark tale. Finally, I did, too.

How could I be even remotely mad? I was having the time of my life, traveling internationally; I was present and enjoying every moment God gave me, finally feeling comfortable in my own skin.

It's a blessing that I am here to share that testimony, and not just because I was addicted and could have died out there on those streets, but because once I got clean and sober and well on my way back to a career and life fulfilled, cancer threatened to do what the drugs could not. I licked the drugs and alcohol, I defeated homelessness, I got on my feet, found love, got myself a new solo career, and turned my entire life around, only to find out that I had prostate cancer.

It was my wife who convinced me to go to the doctor in the first place. I never liked going to physicians because I didn't want to carry the weight that comes with finding out something is wrong. But in the beginning of our relationship, my wife insisted we take good care of ourselves. Later, after I got back on the stage, she wanted to make sure I was in top physical condition to perform in the style I demanded of myself. She had standing doctor's appointments for us every six months, and though I didn't care for them at all, she made sure I made it there. For the longest time, I was fine, but at one particular physical, my doctor insisted that a man my age should be having regular prostate screenings. I fought it—hard. "I don't have cancer," I said casually. "That won't be necessary."

Mahin wasn't having any of that, though. She made the appointment and made sure that I was there, front and center, for my prostate-specific antigen (PSA) examination—a test that measures the blood level of a protein produced by the prostate gland. The higher the PSA level, the more likely it is that a man has cancer in his prostate, the gland that surrounds the neck of the bladder in men. It wasn't the most pleasant experience; part of the testing is a rectal exam to see whether the prostate is a normal size. Really not my cup of tea. But after it was over, I didn't think much about it.

Until the doctor called.

I was on the road performing when the doctor reached out a week after my PSA test. "These numbers," he said in an urgent tone, "are kind of weird. I want to send you to a specialist."

My heart jumped upon hearing that message and I couldn't concentrate on any shows while I waited to get back home to see the specialist. Finally, when I met with him, he did another test on me and, a few days later, summoned me back to the office. Nervous and scared about the implications of this, I kept saying over and over in my mind, "Man, I hope this isn't something crazy." The doctor said he wanted to perform a biopsy on my prostate to determine definitively whether I had cancer.

When I went to do that biopsy, I was scared enough as it was, but when I got to that office and went into the changing room and saw another guy putting on his clothes after his own procedure, I almost lost it. "Did it hurt?" I asked.

"It's going to be just a little bit uncomfortable," said the guy, who told me he was a doctor.

"Be real with me, doc—did it hurt?" I asked again.

He put on his shoes and looked up at me. "It's just going to be a little bit uncomfortable," he said more slowly, deliberately, his voice climbing at the words "little" and "bit."

"Aw man," I exclaimed, "that means it's going to hurt!"

And it did. The technician who conducted the biopsy didn't even want to show me the instrument he was inserting in me. When they went through my rectum and started getting those samples, it was the worst pain that I have ever endured in my entire life. I've been shot (one time, I accidently shot myself when a gun I was carrying in my pocket discharged). I've been cut. But nothing hurt like that biopsy. They were going after twenty-two samples, but they could only get fourteen. I was holding on to that bed rail like, "Dude, you better handcuff me, because if you hit that button one more time, I'm coming up off this table. *One more time.*" Seriously, it felt as if I were being stabbed internally with a butcher knife.

But the worst was yet to come: after it was over and the doctor read the tests, he called me back to the office. "I got some good news and I got some bad news," he said.

"Give us the bad news first," Mahin said.

"The bad news is that you have prostate cancer," he said to me.

Everything—the earth, the very beating of my heart—stood still. That was the worst news I'd heard in my entire life. *Cancer.*

"The good news," the doctor added, "is that it's early and if we go after it right now, we can get it."

To be honest, I really couldn't hear, much less focus on, what he was saying after that. I heard snatches of it—"be positive," "we're going to beat this thing," "do what you're supposed to do." But really, all I could process in my mind was, "I'm going to die with this disease. I'm not going to finish out my career." It felt like this man had given me a death sentence and cancer was going to be my executioner.

The doctor's response to my fear? He gave me a brochure. *A brochure.* "It has all the different options you can consider for treatment," he said simply. "But we have to come up with a plan of action quickly, because your levels between the first and second tests already showed growth. It's moving fast."

By the time I got home and settled down just a little bit, I did look through that brochure and it was much more helpful than I had imagined. After I finished reading it, I got down on my knees and I prayed. "God, I know that I'm a fighter; I've been defying the odds, and we've been fighting together, and I prayed a long time for you not to let the devil kill me out there in the streets and you didn't let that happen. So I'm going to ask, don't let this cancer kill me before I can go and do what it is that I really want to do." And after I got up off my knees praying, I told my wife that I wanted to tell everybody that I have this disease because I wanted them to know how I felt and how I was going to get through it.

As I prepared to fight, I did a little digging and found out that my grandfather had died from it, and my father was battling it, though he hadn't told me. He'd already had it and fought it successfully when he was in his seventies, still pushing himself in the pulpit as I do today onstage. He couldn't jump as high as he used to and he couldn't hit all those notes like before, but he switched it up and did other things. He was powerful. But the cancer, he hid from me. He fought it successfully for years. Yet it came back with a vengeance after he retired, just as I was coming to terms with my own plight with the disease. He tried chemotherapy but it took his hair out and made him feel worse, and he decided he didn't want to fight anymore. "I'm an old man," he said. "I'm not going to be bald and in this therapy in the hospital all the time, with this stuff making me sick."

He fought it mostly on his own. There I was, telling everybody I had prostate cancer, and I didn't know he was suffering from it. I didn't find out about any of this until about a year before he passed away. He was already ninety when the cancer metastasized. There wasn't anything else wrong with him; he was in his right mind, he could still express himself, he could get around well, and he was still doing good works for the people—preaching the gospel, coordinating the collection of clothing for the homeless, all kinds of things. But he looked so small—smaller than I'd ever seen him. And when we took him out to a fancy restaurant for his birthday, he confided in me. "I'm dying, son," he said. "I don't want to die here in California. I want to go south, to Mississippi."

His wife had people down there and so they found them a little house and she cared for him until his dying day. I saw him about a week before he passed, dressed up and in his wheelchair. We sat there at the dinner table in his kitchen where they ate. She'd put his suit on him. Always, he wore a suit and shoes. He loved shoes. One time he was out on the road with us and we put him in a jogging suit and he still had on his dress shoes. He never, ever wore tennis shoes. We would laugh at him, but he didn't pay us any mind. He was who he was. And in the end, that is what mattered. Life, indeed, was for the living.

And so when it came to my cancer, I did what I needed to do to live.

First, I picked the procedure I thought would be best for my prognosis; I selected the surgery. I checked into the hospital and noticed that the nurses were peeping around corners. And just when they were about to put me under, the oncologist came in and said, "Yo, man, you didn't tell me you were *the* Charlie Wilson! Can you sign my CD?"

———

"Doc, are you serious?" I asked.

"I'm serious as a heart attack!" he said, pushing that CD in my face.

I was so out of it I barely got that signature off. And as I was going under, all I remember is the doctor saying he was going to play "You Dropped a Bomb on Me" while he was doing my procedure. When they rolled me in, all the doctors and nurses were singing it.

When I came to, I asked the doc whether he'd played it.

"I rocked The GAP Band loud in there," he said, laughing. "I played it from the top to the bottom, all four hours."

When I came to and was able to go home, my wife was helping me, and when she opened the curtain there were fifteen people standing there, waiting to take pictures and get autographs.

After my ordeal, I started reading up on the disease and making changes to stay healthy. I started avoiding foods that exacerbate it, like corn and charred meat, and started embracing things I didn't necessarily like to eat before, like cauliflower and cooked tomatoes. I cut out eating fatty foods that made me feel sluggish, like fast food, fried food, and things like that. And then I focused on how I could spread the word to men—particularly black men, who are disproportionately affected by prostate cancer—to get checked and treated. Getting cancer—and beating it—changed my life. And I told the world as much when I teamed up with the Prostate Cancer Foundation to take that message to churches, schools, colleges, and seminars all around the country, sharing my journey with men, encouraging them to get tested and take better care of themselves. Men need to know that it's a diagnosis, not a death sentence. Early detection is essential. I could have just not gone back to the doctor and fooled myself into believing that I didn't have cancer, that I wasn't going to die. I know people who've made that choice, too. I once received the Rev. Charles Williams Award, named for a man in Indiana who had a mobile testing truck that he used to park outside the hospital and churches and radio stations so that people could come and get PSA tests. Don't you know he died from prostate cancer? He never got himself tested! The same was true of my own father: he did everything for everybody, but he didn't check himself for prostate cancer until it was much too late. That's how men are—they never talk about their health with anyone, especially with women around. I wanted to break the cycle, first with my family, by talking to my daughters, telling them to tell their sons that this runs in our family and they need to get tested regularly. And then I wanted to spread that same word to the public. I'll continue advocating for it until I get millions of African-American men to take their health seriously and get themselves tested. I've had that responsibility on my shoulders since 2008.

That journey is part of the impetus for one of my songs on the *Love, Charlie* album—a piece Mahin heard and saw in a dream. She came to me one morning and said, "Honey, I had a dream about this song. You recorded it and then it was nominated for a Grammy."

"Wow, really?" I said, a little sarcastically.

"Yes," she said, pulling out a piece of paper. "I wrote it down for you."

I eventually recorded that song, "If I Believe," an inspirational paean to my life journey. My faith in God had everything to do with all that I've overcome, from the addiction to the cancer, and I wanted to honor that the best way I knew how. That song received an incredible reception, but I must admit, I was disappointed when the 2014 Grammy nominations came and "If I Believe" was not among the more obvious categories. "Did you check the gospel category?" Mahin asked simply. Sure enough, there it was, nominated for Best Gospel Song.

I did not win the Grammy for that record, but another blessing did come from it: I was asked to present at the 2014 Grammy Awards ceremony, which led to my reconnection with Jimmy Jam and the fulfillment of my longtime dream of working with him and Terry Lewis on new music. Being a part of the Grammy ceremony also put me in the same space as Susan Rosenbluth of AEG Live and Jeff Sharp, head of AEG's Urban Touring division. We'd been trying for years to get Jeff to put me on the AEG tour roster, but he wouldn't bite. That evening, though, as I sat in the Chairman's Room of the Staples Center in Los Angeles waiting to present an award at the Grammy Awards show, Jeff saw the vision, acknowledged my success, expressed how proud he was of me and my career, and made it clear that he wanted to cut a deal for a Charlie Wilson tour. He was so serious about it that he actually wrote the details for the tour on a cocktail napkin and signed his name at the bottom as a gesture of goodwill. I was blown away in that moment, watching Michael, the young kid who, sixteen years earlier, had been sitting on the floor counting GAP Band money, negotiate the terms. We'd come so far.

Chapter 15

A Place in the Sun

One of the best things I ever did was buy myself a ranch far out-side of Los Angeles, a million miles away, it seemed, from where I'd found trouble. The ranch was beautiful: twenty acres of pasture and mountain and sky and a collection of animals that this old Tulsa boy loves. Mahin, too, found solace there. She's got a deft touch; she taught me how to train baby chicks and ducks.

When we first moved to the ranch, I was intent on filling the farm with exotic animals. Extravagant thoughts of llamas and alpacas quickly turned to thoughts of horses, so we ended up starting our farm with horses instead. I didn't really know how to ride and was a little afraid of them back then after an unfortunate incident years ago when I was on a horse and it just took off from the trail and dashed full speed back to the ranch I was visiting. I had to hold on to the horse's neck because he had his head down and was just going! I didn't want to get on a horse ever again—didn't want to experience that. But if I was going to fill up my ranch with beautiful animals—and get over my fear—horses seemed like the most logical, affordable way to start my collection. I ended up purchasing twelve for my twelve-stall barn, along with all the tools I needed to properly care for the animals: rings, saddles, blankets, and grooming and first-aid supplies. In return, they gave me an intense therapeutic solitude. They calmed my spirit.

Eventually, Mahin and I expanded our farm to include alpacas, llamas, lambs, ostriches, ducks, chickens, and roosters. The chickens were the most challenging to care for. I raised three thousand baby chicks that grew into some of the best chickens and roosters on the market—Americanas and Rhode Island Reds. When they started laying eggs, there were so many we couldn't use all of them for ourselves. We decided to sell them to the local farmer's market, under the moniker Charlie Wilson's Mountain Fresh Farm Eggs. I actually got myself a license and hired a man to crate all the eggs, load them in a refrigeration truck I purchased for the occasion, and sell them for me. I thought it was a stellar idea but Mahin wasn't convinced, particularly one day after we went to the farmer's market to see firsthand just how viable a business it was. I gave my best effort to selling our wares: "Come get your fresh eggs—Uncle Charlie Wilson's Mountain Fresh Farm Eggs!" I was yelling. "You don't want to miss this! Fresh eggs, fresh from the farm. Come on around and get you some! I'm Uncle Charlie and these are my eggs!"

One woman said to her girlfriend, "That's Charlie Wilson over there."

Her friend looked over and shook her head. "That ain't no Charlie Wilson!"

Undeterred, the woman who recognized me asked, "Charlie Wilson, can I take a picture with you?"

"Only if you go right down there and buy some of my eggs," I said.

"Uh-uh, them ain't your eggs!" she said, laughing. "I saw something down there with Uncle Charlie's Fresh Farm Eggs or something. Those your eggs?"

"Yes!" I said insistently.

"Well, let me get on down there and buy some of this man's eggs, then!" she said, rushing off.

She bought five flats! Still, it was a rough business and the amount of work we put into it didn't live up to the promise. By the time my wife tallied up the expenses—the gas, the cost of the truck, food for the chickens, lunch for us and our worker— we'd made a grand total of about thirty dollars. That was the beginning and end of Charlie Wilson's Mountain Fresh Farm Eggs. Instead, we gave the eggs away to the community, and later, we gave away most of the chickens, too.

It was the llamas that taught me a sound lesson about patience. I had about four of them, but one stayed angry with me after I got frustrated one day and went out into their pack yelling, throwing my hands up, and ordering them around. The next day when I went out among them, that llama spit at me. It was the worst smell ever! I disliked the animal's angry attitude, but I learned something in caring for it: I had to learn how to check *my* anger and fix what was wrong with my behavior when I was around him so that he would trust me again. It took me three whole months to make up with that llama, talking calmly and softly to him, coaxing him into eating treats directly from my hand, rubbing his feet with a special long-handled brush. Slowly, I gained his trust. First, he let me brush his legs and back, and then, soon enough, he would greet me near the barn and, after that, the fence. I had to rub a llama's feet for three months to get him to trust me.

That's the story of my life. I can't help but see the parallels between the lifeblood of the ranch and that of my own life, growing and stretching and settling into this quiet existence. While I got those animals to trust me, I learned how to trust myself, figuring out what is worthy of my time and effort, understanding the importance of staying focused and passionate, and also the importance of being gentle with myself. I learned, too, how to forgive myself and get on with life, careful not to get spooked along the way. When you're a recovering addict, this is something you have to do every single day: heal and nurture yourself. Being out with nature was a great way for me to stay in touch with my own feelings while life went on. The only things I heard when I was out walking the property were the sound of my own footsteps and life, the kind that comes when a mare is hitting her hoof on the stall and kicking and letting you know to get back while her baby jumps for joy and reaches for my outstretched hands to touch and taste the wonder of the new. That simple life and the self-care that comes with it have become all that matters to me. Out in nature, I can get with my God and pray, and thank Him for His glory and His mercy and His grace.

This isn't about money, mind you, or how many fancy things I can pile into this lifetime.

· · ·

I am far from a man who is putting himself out to pasture. My greatest love next to God and my wife and children is my craft—

my art. I am overjoyed by the fact that, at this age, I am basking in the bright lights of storied concert halls in front of sold-out audiences who've paid their hard-earned money to see my solo shows. Walking out onto the stage with my band, background singers, and dancers surrounding me and looking out over an excited crowd, swaying and singing to every word and inflection of my songs, is overwhelming—still generates one of the most incredible feelings I've ever had in my life, next to making love to my wife. With six decades under my belt, some of it full of love and wonder, some of it full of hard living and difficult lessons, I've been working every single day to appreciate my second chance. God had his hand on me and kept me living. He knew I would be able to testify one day, and often when I tell my fans the story of my epic downfall and spectacular personal and career resurrection, someone walks up to me after the show, gives me a coin, and says, "I've been clean one year." Other times, someone will walk up to me crying and say, "Man, my father is smoking, and the next time you come, I'm going to bring him. Will you say the same thing you said tonight?" I need to hear this. I never tire of it. Always, I tell them, "I needed that. Give God the praise. Don't ever stop." For me, this is critical—as necessary as air. It was He, after all, who brought me through.

My life is a miracle. And this is just the beginning. My story continues.

Acknowledgments

To my fans, who have stood with me, danced to my music, and sang my songs throughout the years, whether I was performing with The GAP Band or singing on my own: thank you. It is because of you that I am able to continue to make beautiful music.

I would also like to thank Denene Millner for helping me tell the story of my life. We had to go back to some of the darkest times of my journey as a man and musician, and your choice of words and writing made the story come alive.

To my wife, Mahin, thank you for standing by my side every day. You are my inspiration.

To Michael Paran, my manager: you have fought for me since day one and molded my career and life into something of which I could never have dreamed. But you are so much more to me than a manager; you are my son, and I am grateful for you every day. You helped pave the way for my comeback story and we continue to defy the odds together. I can't wait to see what more God has in store for us.

And to Jenna Lankford, from my management team: thank you for taking the time to go through this book with me. Your hard work is always appreciated.

Acknowledgments

To Mark Siegel and Dan Kirschen at ICM: thank you for taking the journey with me on this new endeavor.

I'm grateful, too, for Simon & Schuster and 37 INK, particularly my editor, Dawn Davis, for believing in my story and making my dream of publishing my own book a reality, and Yona Deshommes for seeing the vision and helping me share my story with the world.

God, you are so good. I want to thank you for all of the blessings you have bestowed upon me in my life. I will always give you the praise.

Index

Index